Happiness Through Goal Setti

An evidence-based, practical guide to reflection on the most important goals in life, this book provides a unique framework and thought-provoking exercises to modify personal and professional goals to increase happiness.

Why we pursue our most important goals in life is an important question, and the answer we give ourselves greatly influences our happiness. This book presents the goal-striving reasons framework to illustrate the essential positive and negative ingredients: pleasure, altruism, self-esteem, and necessity. This new framework and the practical exercises throughout the book will enable readers to change their reasons for pursuing goals and achieve the ultimate aim of becoming happier in life.

There are many books on happiness – no other discusses happiness specifically from a goal-setting perspective. Human resources and mental health professionals, mindfulness practitioners, coaches, mentors, higher education staff, postgraduate students, and others will benefit from the hands-on guidance in this book.

Christian Ehrlich completed his PhD at the University of Kaiserslautern on work motivation. He is currently working at Oxford Brookes Business School. His research interests are around goals and happiness, where he developed the goal-striving reasons framework on which the "Happiness through Goal Setting" training is based.

Sashenka Milston is an Executive Team Coach. She also continues to lecture at Oxford Brookes Business School. She has taught at universities and colleges in Australia and the UK and trained and coached teams and individuals internationally. Sashenka holds a PhD in Psychology.

"If there was ever a time for the pursuit of happiness, it's now. This book encourages you to reflect on the reasons behind your goal setting and explains how you might reconsider those reasons to find happiness."

Dian Harvey, *Psychotherapist, UK*

"I have found this book so helpful! The authors guide you progressively through a reflection on what really lies beneath your life goals, using all the latest evidence. I use the approach for myself and in career development coaching at work."

Professor Helen Walkington, *Oxford Brookes University, UK*

"For anyone lacking in career or life direction, some insightful ideas and practical activities designed to question choices which may not sing from the heart. A holistic approach to goal setting through looking at achievement through a very different lens."

Emma Robinson, *Careers Consultant, Oxford Brookes University, UK*

"This book is offering a practical and research-based framework to coaches, mentors, line managers, coach educators and anybody else involved in developing others for crafting more meaningful goals. I am using the ideas and exercises in this book with my coaching clients who found they are highly motivated to work on their goals and the approach benefits their well-being. Being more focussed on their learning instead of performance liberates them to find new resources to fulfil their potential and achieve their goals. Personally, having used the goal-striving framework as a self-coaching tool for some time now, my business has benefited immensely as I am aligning the business goals with my overall life goals, hence making them more sustainable."

Claudia Filsinger, *Executive Coach and Coaching Supervisor at Moving Maps Ltd, Associate of the International Centre for Coaching and Mentoring Studies at Oxford Brookes University, UK*

Happiness Through Goal Setting

A Practical Guide to Reflect on and Change the Reasons Why You Pursue Your Most Important Goals in Life

Christian Ehrlich and Sashenka Milston

Routledge
Taylor & Francis Group

NEW YORK AND LONDON

First published 2022
by Routledge
605 Third Avenue, New York, NY 10158

and by Routledge
2 Park Square, Milton Park, Abingdon, Oxon, OX14 4RN

Routledge is an imprint of the Taylor & Francis Group, an informa business

Library of Congress Cataloging-in-Publication Data
Names: Ehrlich, Christian, author. | Milston, Sashenka, author.
Title: Happiness through goal setting : a practical guide to reflect on and change the reasons why you pursue your most important goals in life / Christian Ehrlich and Sashenka Milston.
Description: New York : Routledge, 2021. | Includes bibliographical references and index.
Identifiers: LCCN 2021005760 (print) | LCCN 2021005761 (ebook)
Subjects: LCSH: Goal (Psychology) | Self-actualization (Psychology) | Happiness.
Classification: LCC BF503 .E417 2021 (print) | LCC BF503 (ebook) | DDC 158--dc23
LC record available at https://lccn.loc.gov/2021005760
LC ebook record available at https://lccn.loc.gov/2021005761

ISBN: 9781032002316 (hbk)
ISBN: 9781032002309 (pbk)
ISBN: 9781003173250 (ebk)

Typeset in Sabon
by Deanta Global Publishing Services Chennai India

Contents

Part 1

The big picture

Chapter 1

Introduction

This book is focused on one fundamental question: why do you pursue your most important goals in life? This question is an important one because research has shown that the answers you give yourself matter to your happiness. So, we might as well ensure that we are pursuing our most important goals for the right or best possible reasons. But what are the right or best possible reasons? And are there any wrong reasons? This book, based on empirical evidence, identifies two happiness-increasing reasons to pursue one's goals and two happiness-decreasing ones. It also contains effective strategies to help you either change your goals or the reasons for pursuing them, with the ultimate purpose of making yourself happier.

To give you a quick overview of the four reasons the book focuses on, here is a brief explanation of each. The first positive reason for pursuing your goals is that you really enjoy what you are doing. "Well, that's fairly obvious", you might be thinking. And you would be right. But it does beg the question, why aren't more people enjoying the goals they are striving for? It seems evident when we look around – or maybe even at ourselves – that quite often, or even far too often, people are doing things that they do not really enjoy. So, the challenging quest behind this first reason is figuring out how to pursue important goals that are also enjoyable. Increasing the amount of enjoyment within our goal pursuit can enhance happiness. The second positive reason for pursuing a goal is that we feel it helps others or it makes the world a better place. Helping others is one of the most powerful things we can do to make ourselves happy. However, one of the most crucial goal-reasons that hinders us from becoming happy is doing things to prove our self-worth. If we strive for certain goals because we need to (constantly) validate ourselves, then this stands in the way of our happiness. Finally, doing things out of necessity can also detract from our happiness. We all have to do some things in life that we do not particularly like, but there is an ever-present danger of doing too many things we do not like, and so it is worthwhile reflecting on them and checking if they are truly necessary.

We believe that you will get the most out of this book by applying the information about "happy goals" to your own goals. So, a good way to kick things off is to state your four most important goals in life/work in Table 1.1. Remember, they are not set in stone and could even change as you work through the book. But it is difficult to work out if you are on the right path or if you require a course correction unless you know your current location. There is also space in the table to jot down the reasons why you are striving for each of your goals. This will be useful for reflecting on those reasons as you work through the book.

Table 1.1 Your most important goals

My most important goal is	
The reason(s) why I strive for my most important goal is/are	
My second most important goal is	
The reason(s) why I strive for my second most important goal is/are	
My third most important goal is	
The reason(s) why I strive for my third most important goal is/are	
My fourth most important goal is	
The reason(s) why I strive for my fourth most important goal is/are	

Chapter 2

Why happiness matters

Happiness is seen by both researchers and lay-people as an ultimate goal in life. This is evident by the number of research papers, books, forums, and websites dedicated to the topic. Indeed, for many, the state of being happy is a central criterion for living a fulfilling life.

It is also not just a Western phenomenon (Lyubomirsky, Sheldon, & Schkade, 2005). Happiness is now seen as a global issue, with people around the world seeing happiness as an important aspect of their lives. So much so that the United Nations has recognised happiness as a universal right of humans. In 2012, the UN convened the inaugural annual meeting on happiness, bringing together global data on national happiness levels and reviewing evidence from the science of happiness, and officially declared the 20th of March as the International Day of Happiness.

All of this is for a good reason: happiness brings a multitude of benefits in multiple domains. In an exhaustive review of all available happiness research, Lyubomirsky, King, and Diener (2005) examined experimental, longitudinal, and correlational data from over 275,000 people. They found that happiness can lead to positive effects on our performance (e.g., increased productivity and quality of work), health (e.g., more energy, better immunity, lower stress and pain levels, longer life), relationships (e.g., longer and more satisfying marriages, more friends with richer interactions and greater social support), and society as a whole with more helpful and charitable behaviour. Ed Diener, another leading researcher in the field of happiness, supports the message and suggests that the evidence is "clear and compelling" (Diener & Chan, 2011, p. 33) that happiness influences health and longevity.

Shawn Achor writes about a fundamental truth in his book, *The Happiness Advantage* (2011), and this may be one of the most important messages. We are taught to believe that if we work hard, we will be successful, which will then make us happy. However,

> the formula is broken because it is backward. More than a decade of ground-breaking research … has proven in no uncertain terms that …

happiness is the precursor to success, not merely the result. And that happiness and optimism actually *fuel* performance and achievement.

(Achor, 2011, p. 3)

Most importantly, the fact that you are holding this book in your hand right now means happiness matters to you.

References

Achor, S. (2011). *The happiness advantage: The seven principles of positive psychology that fuel success and performance at work*. London: Virgin Books.

Diener, E., & Chan, M. Y. (2011). Happy people live longer: Subjective well-being contributes to health and longevity. *Applied Psychology: Health and Well-Being, 3*(1), 1–43. doi: 10.1111/j.1758-0854.2010.01045.x

Lyubomirsky, S., King, L. A., & Diener, E. (2005). The benefits of frequent positive affect: Does happiness lead to success? *Psychological Bulletin, 131*(6), 803–855. doi: 10.1037/0033-2909.131.6.803

Lyubomirsky, S., Sheldon, K. M., & Schkade, D. (2005). Pursuing happiness: The architecture of sustainable change. *Review of General Psychology, 9*(2), 111–131. doi: 10.1037/1089-2680.9.2.111

Chapter 3

Things to consider on your happiness journey, including a word of warning

If you have picked up this book with the ultimate aim of leading a happier life, or even just finding a few new ideas, then this chapter may help you with some general knowledge and guidance. It touches on the three key aspects around happiness which are important to keep in mind when modifying your reasons behind goal pursuit and apply to any changes you make to become happier.

Intentional activities and life circumstances – two areas for long-term happiness

There are many strategies for increasing happiness. Lyubomirsky (2007) suggests there are around 200! However, while some are well-researched, others are more mythical in nature. This book primarily focuses on the importance of goals, along with various strategies that can be applied to your goals, none of them mythical in nature!

To set the scene and provide a little background explanation, we will start on a broader level. Research suggests that there are three key areas that influence our happiness: our biological set point, the circumstances we are in, and intentional activities (Lyubomirsky, Sheldon, & Schkade, 2005). This original research gave rise to the sustainable happiness model and suggested that our genes (biological set point) influence our long-term happiness by up to 50%. There is not much we can do about this factor. Our circumstances, such as how much money we earn, the house we live in, etc., contribute 10%. The remaining 40% is determined by our intentional activities – things we can do to improve our happiness that do not happen on their own and require some effort. Goals are subsumed under this category.

The model was academically critiqued and the 40% attribution to intentional activities was suggested to be overestimated (see Brown & Rohrer, 2019). In response, Sheldon and Lyubomirsky (2019) agreed that it was difficult to quantify the influence of those three factors. However, they stood behind the central premise of their model and successfully demonstrated that long-term happiness is possible by continued, wilful effort in eudaimonic-type activities (growth-promoting goals and intentional behaviours). At the same time, they also added that the 10% for circumstances might, at times, be higher. They discussed some key processes that significantly influence the degree to which circumstances impact on our long-term happiness. They (still) acknowledged that circumstances are, as previously argued, subject to hedonic adaptation – we get used to things as they become routine and subsequently have less of a boost out of them, no longer feeling the same level of enjoyment. This is why their original estimate of circumstances was so low. However, they now propose that there are things people can do to prevent hedonic adaptation and therefore make circumstances a more powerful tool to improve long-term happiness than previously thought. Although circumstances are not the key focus of this book, we wanted to briefly mention the key messages that can be drawn from research to make the most out of one's circumstances. One method is a bottom-up approach and the other is top-down (Sheldon & Lyubomirsky, 2019). The bottom-up approach states that individuals who experience positive circumstantial change need to continue interacting with it in a variety of different ways. For example, if someone buys a bigger house, then the individual needs to make regular, positive use of this in a variety of ways, such as inviting friends over for dinner parties, decorating it for the seasonal holidays, redecorating or moving furniture around to make different use of the space, making friends with the neighbours, etc. The initial purchase supplies the happiness boost, but the varied use of it sustains it. The second route to prevent hedonic adaptation, top-down, is to avoid wanting even more of the same change (e.g., an even bigger house). These kinds of aspirations put a downer on our long-term happiness. For example, as soon as one starts thinking about the next house, the ability to get enjoyment out of the current house is reduced. Instead, one needs to continue to focus on and intentionally appreciate what they currently have. This is very much linked to literature showing the negative impact of materialism on happiness and the desire to acquire more and more, as will be discussed in detail in Chapter 5. However, the general premise is that we seem to be genetically programmed to continually want more stuff. Russ Harris explains the idea well in his book, *The Happiness Trap* (2008, p. 5):

> Now, for any Stone Age person with ambition, the general rule for success is: get more, get better. The better your weapons, the more food you can kill. The larger your food stores, the greater your chances are for survival in times of scarcity. The better your shelter, the safer you are from weather and wild animals. The more children you have, the greater the chance that some will survive into adulthood. No surprise then that our modern mind continually looks for "more and better": more money, a better job, more status, a better body, more love, a better partner. And if we succeed, if we actually do get more money or a

better car or a better-looking body, then we're satisfied – for a while. But sooner or later (and usually sooner), we end up wanting more.

In essence, we have been shaped by evolution to never get complacent and to constantly evaluate our situation in our fight for survival. As a result, it is difficult to be content with what we have and to find lasting happiness.

Happiness requires constant fuelling

The idea of the successful pursuit of happiness requires awareness, knowledge, and intentional buy-in by participants (Sheldon & Lyubomirsky, 2019). Lyubomirsky et al. (2011) found the biggest boosts to sustained happiness occurred for participants who a) wanted to change and b) applied sufficient effort in c) meaningful activities.

As mentioned in the previous section, these efforts need to be ongoing. "A steady flow of positive experiences … that interest, inspire, connect, and uplift" need to be created and nurtured on a more or less daily basis (Sheldon & Lyubomirsky, 2019, p. 5). It can be compared to a log fire that needs constant fuelling to prevent it from dying down. Not everyone is willing to make this effort. Are you?

Constantly fuelling the fire requires setting time aside, making an effort, and most importantly, sticking to it over a prolonged period of time. However, as you may remember, at the beginning of this book we asked you to write down your four most important goals. We did not need to tell you what they are – they are yours – they are a reflection of what is important to you. So, because those goals are important to you, you are already working on them. Thus, we would argue, you do not need to set any further time aside or make any further effort than you are already. This book is simply providing you with some information on how to work on your goals in a more powerful way that can make you happier. Goals give us the opportunity to come back to goal-related activities that (if we have chosen them correctly) provide us with the opportunity to fuel our own fire (in our hearts) again and again and hopefully never tire of.

Valuing happiness – can this be a bad thing?

Undoubtedly, happiness interventions have demonstrated a positive effect on people's happiness (Seligman et al., 2005). Deliberately seeking positivity and prioritising it has been shown to increase happiness and reduce depression (Catalino et al., 2014). However, can placing too much focus and value on the outcome – being happy – cause people to be less happy?

In fact, some studies suggest such a negative association between valuing and experiencing happiness does exist, whereby placing excessive value on one's happiness and having the desire to be as happy as possible as often as possible is associated with negative psychological health such as depression (see Kahriz et al., 2019). Generally speaking, people are more likely to experience negative emotions when there is a societal expectation that they should not feel those negative emotions (Bastian et al., 2012). One of the reasons for this, among others, is the fact that people become very sensitive (hypervigilant) to positive and negative events, internally and externally. In this case, the attention bias, i.e., the tendency of people to focus more strongly on negative events than positive events in combination with the strong expectation to be happy, tends to lead people to feel sadder, therefore leading to increasing amounts of negative psychological health. In other words, focusing purely on happiness as an expected end goal can, at times, result in lower life satisfaction.

Keeping in mind the negative effects of overly focussing on being happy as an end state, the recommendation therefore is to move your focus away from the overall end goal of becoming happy and instead to focus on the process or the actions you are taking to become happier. It could be compared to losing weight. Standing on the scales every five minutes, searching for that elusive end goal, and getting upset that you are not there yet, is probably not the most effective method of losing weight! It is far better to engage in the exercise and dieting activities for which weight loss is a by-product. Another example is every small child who jumps in a puddle. They do not jump in the puddle because they want to be happy; they do it out of curiosity and fun, while the joy they feel from the activity is simply the by-product.

Finally, it is also important to remember that negative emotions are part of our lives – even for generally happy people. "Happy people are able to react with negative emotions when it is appropriate to do so" (Lyubomirsky, King, & Diener, 2005, p. 846). Indeed, experiencing emodiversity – the variety and abundance of human emotions – has been shown to enhance both mental and physical health (Quoidbach et al., 2014).

Thus, to conclude this chapter, one of the key messages from the research is that happiness should be the natural by-product of our actions and behaviours. We should not chase after positive emotions directly – but enjoy them when they arrive because of what we did. Happiness is not a destination, but instead the path.

References

Bastian, B., Kuppens, P., Hornsey, M. J., Park, J., Koval, P., & Uchida, Y. (2012). Feeling bad about being sad: The role of social expectancies in amplifying negative mood. *Emotion, 12*(1), 69–80. doi: 10.1037/a0024755

Brown, N. J. L., & Rohrer, J. M. (2019). Easy as (happiness) pie? A critical evaluation of a popular model of the determinants of well-being. *Journal of Happiness Studies: An Interdisciplinary Forum on Subjective Well-Being, 21*(4), 1285–1301. doi: 10.1007/s10902-019-00128-4

Catalino, L. I., Algoe, S. B., & Fredrickson, B. L. (2014). Prioritizing positivity: An effective approach to pursuing happiness? *Emotion*, 14(6), 1155–1161. doi: 10.1037/a0038029

Harris, R. (2008) *The happiness trap*. London: Robinson Publishing.

Kahriz, B. M., Bower, J. L., Glover, F. M. G. Q., & Vogt, J. (2019). Wanting to be happy but not knowing how: Poor attentional control and emotion-regulation abilities mediate the association between valuing happiness and depression. *Journal of Happiness Studies*, 21(7), 2583–2601. doi: 10.1007/s10902-019-00193-9

Lyubomirsky, S. (2007). *The how of happiness: A scientific approach to getting the life you want*. New York: Penguin Press.

Lyubomirsky, S., Dickerhoof, R., Boehm, J. K., & Sheldon, K. M. (2011). Becoming happier takes both a will and a proper way: An experimental longitudinal intervention to boost well-being. *Emotion*, 11(2), 391–402.

Lyubomirsky, S., King, L. A., & Diener, E. (2005). The benefits of frequent positive affect: Does happiness lead to success? *Psychological Bulletin*, 131(6), 803–855. doi: 10.1037/0033-2909.131.6.803

Lyubomirski, S., Sheldon, K. M., & Schkade, D. (2005). Pursuing happiness: The architecture of sustainable change. *Review of General Psychology*, 9(2), 111–131. doi: 10.1037/1089-2680.9.2.111

Quoidbach, J., Gruber, J., Mikolajczak, M., Kogan, A., Kotsou, I., & Norton, M. I. (2014). Emodiversity and the emotional ecosystem. *Journal of Experimental Psychology: General*, 143(6), 2057–2066. doi: 10.1037/a0038025

Seligman, M. E. P., Steen, T. A., Park, N., & Peterson, C. (2005). Positive psychology progress: Empirical validation of interventions. *American Psychologist*, 60(5), 410–421. doi: 10.1037/0003-066X.60.5.410

Sheldon, K. M., & Lyubomirsky, S. (2019). Revisiting the sustainable happiness model and pie chart: Can happiness be successfully pursued? *The Journal of Positive Psychology*. Advance online publication. doi: 10.1080/17439760.2019.1689421

Chapter 4

Why goals matter for our happiness

As we saw in the last chapter, "intentional activities" are one of the most important things we can do to increase our long-term happiness. One powerful strategy in this domain is working on our goals. Goals have the advantage that, compared to other intentional activities, people generally already have goals. Even those who say that they do not have goals still want things in life or have an idea of how they would like their life to develop. If we broadly define goals as simply what people want in life, then most people already have at least one goal.

However, our personal experience about people and their relationship to goals seems somehow complex and at times counterintuitive. This is mostly because although many people would agree with the notion that goals are important and to an extent goals give people something to focus on and structure their daily lives, many people do not actually spend much time reflecting on their goals (Frese & Zapf, 1994). Indeed, in relation to people's career goals, John Lees (2013/2014, p. 256), a well-known career coach, even remarks that we probably "spend more time planning our annual holiday, car purchase or our new kitchen than we spend thinking about our career" (goals) and whether they are right for us. The question therefore remains, why is this the case?

The answer is mainly that people do not realise that more careful consideration of our goals is needed due to a lack of knowledge on what actually does and doesn't make us happy. Many people might have the assumption that the goals they have are the things that they want in life and that achieving them will make them happy. One might think, "How can what I want from life be wrong or maybe not an ideal contribution to my happiness?" In fact, there is clear evidence that certain characteristics of goals are stronger contributors to happiness than others. For example, Kasser and Ryan (1993; 1996) showed that goals focussed on self-acceptance and community are more strongly associated with happiness than goals focussed on financial success (see Chapter 9). Equally, a substantial amount of research has clearly demonstrated that goals whereby people work towards the achievement of a desirable outcome (approach motivation) are a stronger contributor to people's happiness than goals whereby people work towards the avoidance of an undesirable outcome (avoidance motivation; Dickson, 2006; Elliot & Sheldon, 1997; Ryan & Deci, 2001; also see Chapter 5). Finally, people might think that it does not really matter what goals they have – as long as they achieve them, this will make them happy. However, again, research has clearly shown that people who achieve goals that fit with their personality report greater happiness than people who attained goals that did not fit with their personality (Sheldon & Elliot, 1999; Sheldon, 2014). Thus, this strand of research strongly indicates that one needs to reflect carefully about one's goals and how they fit with oneself. One reason for this tendency could be that we make decisions based on how we think we will feel once we have achieved our goals. However, we tend to overestimate the intensity and duration of our future (positive – but also negative) emotions from present events (Wilson & Gilbert, 2005). All of this makes us terrible judges all around on what will and will not make us happy and to what extent!

To sum up, research has shown that it is not simply about achieving goals: it is more about setting and pursuing the right goals. This, essentially, is what this book is all about. It gives you the knowledge to help you make the best choices about your goals, with the ultimate aim of helping you lead a happier life. It does this by going one step further, or indeed deeper. This book is less concerned with what your goals are, i.e., what it is that you want to achieve. Instead, it is more about the underlying reasons behind your goals. Therefore, it asks the question, "**Why** do you want to achieve each of your goals?" Not least because this is a level of goal analysis that has received less attention in the public, but from a research point has been shown to be at least an equally important level of goal analysis as the goal itself (Sheldon et al., 2004), if not an even greater one (Carver & Baird, 1998; Ehrlich & Bipp, 2016).

References

Carver, C. S., & Baird, E. (1998). The American dream revisited: Is it what you want or why you want it that matters? *Psychological Science*, 9(4), 289–292. doi: 10.1111/1467-9280.00057

Dickson, J. M. (2006). Perceived consequences underlying approach goals and avoidance goals in relation to anxiety. *Personality and Individual Differences*, 41(8), 1527–1538. doi: 10.1016/j.paid.2006.06.005

Ehrlich, C., & Bipp, T. (2016). Goals and subjective well-being: Further evidence for goal-striving reasons as an additional level of goal analysis. *Personality and Individual Differences*, 89, 92–99. doi: 10.1016/j.paid.2015.10.001

Elliot, A. J., & Sheldon, K. M. (1997). Avoidance achievement motivation: A personal goals analysis. *Journal of Personality and Social Psychology*, 73(1), 171–185. doi: 10.1037/0022-3514.73.1.171

Frese, M., & Zapf, D. (1994). Action as the core of work psychology: A German approach. In H. C. Triandis, M. D. Dunnette, & L. M. Hough (Eds.), *Handbook of industrial and organizational psychology* (pp. 271–340). Palo Alto, CA: Consulting Psychologists Press.

Kasser, T., & Ryan, R. M. (1993). A dark side of the American dream: Correlates of financial success as a central life aspiration. *Journal of Personality and Social Psychology*, 65(2), 410–422. doi: 10.1037/0022-3514.65.2.410

Kasser, T., & Ryan, R. M. (1996). Further examining the American dream: Differential correlates of intrinsic and extrinsic goals. *Personality and Social Psychology Bulletin*, 22(3), 280–287. doi: 10.1177/0146167296223006

Lees, J. (2013/14). *How to get a job you'll love*. London: McGraw-Hill.

Ryan, R. M., & Deci, E. L. (2001). On happiness and human potentials: A review of research on hedonic and eudaimonic well-being. *Annual Review of Psychology*, 52, 141–166. doi: 10.1146/annurev.psych.52.1.141

Sheldon, K. M. (2014). Becoming oneself: The central role of self-concordant goal selection. *Personality and Social Psychology Review*, 18(4), 1–17. doi: 10.1177/1088868314538549

Sheldon, K. M., & Elliot, A. J. (1999). Goal striving, need satisfaction, and longitudinal well-being: The self-concordance model. *Journal of Personality and Social Psychology*, 76(3), 482–497.

Sheldon, K. M., Ryan, R. M., Deci, E. L., & Kasser, T. (2004). The independent effects of goal contents and motives on well-being: It's both what you pursue and why you pursue it. *Personality and Social Psychology Bulletin*, 30(4), 475–486. doi: 10.1177/0146167203261883

Wilson, T. D., & Gilbert, D. T. (2005). Affective forecasting: Knowing what to want. *Current Directions in Psychological Science*, 14(3), 131–134. doi: 10.1111/j.0963-7214.2005.00355.x

Part 2

The four reasons

Chapter 5

What makes for happy goals?

The goal-striving reasons framework

This book is based on the goal-striving reasons framework (Ehrlich, 2012; 2018; 2019; 2020; Ehrlich & Bipp, 2016), a concept which analyses the quality of people's reasons for goal pursuit based on two characteristics. The first characteristic is whether a person pursues a goal out of approach or avoidance reasons. The distinction between approach/avoidance motivation is one of the most influential concepts within motivation psychology as well as goal-setting theory (Elliot & Thrash, 2010; Latham, 2012). This distinction captures whether a person wants to achieve something positive (approach reason) or wants to avoid something negative happening (avoidance reason). For example, an employee might want to complete a work project successfully because this will lead to new opportunities and even more interesting work projects. Equally, someone might want to complete their work project successfully to avoid losing their job – a very avoidance-driven motivation. As you can see, both have the same goal – the successful completion of the project – but one with an approach reason and the other one with an avoidance reason. Research has shown that approach motivation is associated with higher levels of happiness than avoidance motivation (Dickson, 2006; Ryan & Deci, 2001), which is why the distinction between approach/avoidance reasons is also an important distinction for goal reasons (Ehrlich, 2012; 2018).

In addition to the approach/avoidance dimension, the goal-striving reasons framework further distinguishes between approach/avoidance reasons: whether the reasons for goal pursuit are aimed at consequences to the person themself or aimed at changing an external situation. This distinction was first introduced by Ford and Nichols (1987) but also used by many others (Austin & Vancouver, 1996; Eccles & Wigfield, 2002; Ford, 1992). The decision to distinguish between reasons aimed at the person themself or at the external situation is based on the following two factors. Firstly, it acknowledges the fact that an important characteristic of our reasons for goal pursuit should go beyond the immediate benefits for ourselves and therefore should include the consequences for others. Equally, we are not operating in self-isolation but in relation to our environment. This sometimes comes with the necessity to do certain things to be able to make a living.

Based on these arguments, the goal-striving reasons framework claims that there are four core reasons that matter for our happiness (see Figure 5.1). Two of these reasons have been found to be associated with increased happiness. These are:

1. Doing things because we enjoy the pursuit of the goals (pleasure).
2. We feel the pursuit of our goals helps others or makes the world a better place (altruism).

There are also two reasons that lead to a decrease in happiness:

1. Pursuing our goals to prove to ourselves that we are worthy; to maintain a positive view about ourselves (self-esteem).
2. Pursuing our goals because we feel that we must, to be able to make a living; to make ends meet (necessity).

Figure 5.1 The goal-striving reasons framework (adapted from Ehrlich, 2012).

The following chapters will give more background information on each of the four reasons and describe strategies with which to increase the motivational power of the positive ones and decrease the power of the negative ones. If you feel that a particular reason is currently more important than others, then, obviously, feel free to start with that one. However, while no individual goal reason is more important than any other, the four reasons are presented in a natural sequence, so if you wanted to work on all four reasons, plus assertiveness as an enabler, we would recommend the following order:

1. Self-esteem (Chapter 6): This is the best reason to start with if you wanted to work on all four goal-striving reasons. This is because self-esteem is quite often associated with a fear of failure, which can often put shackles on our goals or aspirations. The more we free ourselves from these shackles, the more opportunities we are able to see and take. This definitely has a positive impact on our goals as well as other goal-striving reasons. For example, if our self-esteem is "on the line", then it is quite likely that we are not enjoying what we are doing. Thus, reducing conditional self-esteem will often help with increasing the amount of pleasure in our goal-striving reasons. Additionally, being overly concerned about our own self-esteem also makes it less likely for us to pursue goals for reasons that aim to make the world a better place for others. Finally, the section on self-esteem also promotes the idea of self-compassion, which is another important ingredient for happy and healthy goals.

2. Pleasure (Chapter 7): After working through self-esteem, which is all about reducing some of the negative forces in us, it is then a good time to investigate the idea of increasing the positive forces within us. How can we enjoy more of what we do in relation to our life in general but also in relation to our goals?

3. Altruism (Chapter 8): The next positive force for our happiness to consider is then "doing good for others". Based on the old saying, "You cannot pour from an empty cup", it is therefore good to work on altruism after working on pleasure. Whereas pleasure is more about yourself, altruism is about others or society as a whole.

4. Necessity (Chapter 9): Finally, it is also important to think about how much we can free ourselves from thoughts around material wealth and maybe reflect on issues such as "how much of my goal-strivings are based around the need to gain material wealth?" and "how much of this material wealth do I really need?" The section on necessity aims to provide a great opportunity for reflection on this issue as you determine the answers to those questions for yourself.

5. Assertiveness (Chapter 10): Although this is not a goal reason, it is a necessary quality that underpins everything. If you want to make changes to your goals, then you probably need to negotiate with others regarding how you pursue the goals in the way you want to pursue them. If you are not naturally an assertive person, this may in fact be a good starting point.

For each of the four goal-striving reasons, we also provide strategies and exercises on how to work on each reason. These are not necessarily the only possible ways to work on each goal-striving reason, but they are the ones we consider the most valuable.

References

Austin, J. T., & Vancouver, J. B. (1996). Goal constructs in psychology: Structure, process, and content. *Psychological Bulletin, 120*(3), 338–375. doi: 10.1037/0033-2909.120.3.338

Dickson, J. M. (2006). Perceived consequences underlying approach goals and avoidance goals in relation to anxiety. *Personality and Individual Differences, 41*(8), 1527–1538. doi: 10.1016/j.paid.2006.06.005

Eccles, J. S., & Wigfield, A. (2002). Motivational beliefs, values and goals. *Annual Review of Psychology, 53*(1), 109–132. doi: 10.1146/annurev.psych.53.100901 .135153

Ehrlich, C. (2012). Be careful what you wish for but also why you wish for it: Goal-striving reasons and affective subjective well-being. *Journal of Positive Psychology, 7*(6), 493–503.

Ehrlich, C. (2018). The development of an extended goal-striving reasons framework: Evidence for its relevance in the workplace, for its theoretical difference to self-concordance and for its buffering effect on work intensity. *Journal of Positive Psychology and Wellbeing, 2*(2), 1–23.

Ehrlich, C. (2019). The goal-striving reasons framework: Further evidence for its predictive power for subjective well-being on a sub-dimensional level and on an individual goal-striving reasons level as well as evidence for its theoretical difference to self-concordance. *Current Psychology, Online First*, 1–14. DOI: 10.1007/s12144-019-0158-y

Ehrlich, C. (2020). Development of the short form of the goal-striving reasons questionnaire. *Journal of Well-Being Assessment, 4*(2), 75–94. DOI: 10.1007/ s41543-020-00027-z

Ehrlich, C., & Bipp, T. (2016). Goals and subjective well-being: Further evidence for goal-striving reasons as an additional level of goal analysis. *Personality and Individual Differences, 89*, 92–99. doi: 10.1016/j.paid.2015.10.001

Elliot, A. J., & Thrash, T. M. (2010). Approach and avoidance temperament as basic dimensions of personality. *Journal of Personality, 78*, 865–906. doi: 10.1111/j.1467-6494.2010.00636.x

Ford, I. (1992). *Human motivation: Goals, emotions, and personal agency beliefs.* Newbury Park, CA: SAGE.

Ford, M. E., & Nichols, C. W. (1987). A taxonomy of human goals and some possible applications. In M. E. Ford & D. H. Ford (Eds.), *Humans as self-constructing systems: Putting the framework to work* (pp. 289–311). Hillsdale, NJ: Erlbaum.

Latham, G. P. (2012). *Work motivation. History, theory, research, and practice* (2nd ed.). Los Angeles, CA: Sage Publications.

Ryan, R. M., & Deci, E. L. (2001). On happiness and human potentials: A review of research on hedonic and eudaimonic well-being. *Annual Review of Psychology, 52*, 141–166. doi: 10.1146/annurev.psych.52.1.141

Chapter 6

Self-esteem

Goals that you pursue for self-esteem reasons

We all need and want to think positively about ourselves, and this is essentially what self-esteem is all about: how we judge ourselves. When we look into the mirror, do we like the person we see looking back at ourselves and do we think they are a good person? This is a fundamental human need that we are compelled to satisfy. However, how we satisfy this need – how we arrive at the conclusion that the person in the mirror is okay – is crucial. Generally speaking, there are two ways of thinking about one's self-esteem. People can adopt either a conditional view or an unconditional view about themselves and their self-esteem. The first one needs constant validation: people need to be successful to feel good about themselves. Each time they are successful, self-esteem and happiness boosts occur. However, the flip side to this is that each time they fail in their goals, their self-esteem and happiness is compromised. Unfortunately, failure is a fact of life; it is part of the learning process on the way to becoming successful. Hence, a conditional view of self-esteem always comes with the constant threat of failing in the next task ahead and therefore feeling bad about oneself, rendering any self-esteem and happiness boost as purely short term. This, as you can imagine, comes with higher levels of anxiety, higher levels of stress, and is not good for our long-term mental health. Crocker and Knight (2005) concluded that the negative long-term consequences of conditional self-esteem far outweigh its short-term benefits. As such, an unconditional view of oneself would seem to be the better option. We need to learn to accept and like ourselves despite our flaws and imperfections, or the fact that we get things wrong or fail sometimes. But how do we do that?

We need to challenge the thought of only being happy once we succeed in things. Unconditional self-esteem takes various forms, but here are some comments and thoughts that capture the idea of unconditional self-esteem:

1) Becoming our own friend: We need to start becoming our own best friend, rather than our own worst critic. Interestingly, people tend to speak to themselves in a very harsh way, and often in such a way that they would not even talk to their worst enemy! But, for some reason, we

seem to believe or accept that it is okay to speak to ourselves like that. If it is possible to become comfortable with other people's shortcomings and vulnerabilities and like them for who they are, surely we can learn to do the same with ourselves.

2) Love yourself despite the things you are not: We need to start to consciously love ourselves despite our flaws and imperfections. This is challenging but absolutely worthwhile. For example, not having a university degree, "So what? That does not define my value as a human being, and I am okay despite not having a university degree." This does not mean that one should not try to get a degree if one feels that it is a good thing to have, but if you do get it, it should be because it makes sense to fulfil one's potential in this world, rather than to feel proud and valuable. Think about the reasons for things rather than letting them define you.

3) Being a perfectionist: Another interesting thought regarding unconditional self-esteem is the issue of perfectionism. In many cases, the word "perfectionism" is just a better sounding label for conditional self-esteem. When people call themselves a "perfectionist", do they really want to be perfect (an impossible feat) or are they just afraid of failure because that would threaten their self-esteem? To make matters worse, this fear of failure can then motivate them to continue pursuing perfectionism. However, this kind of motivation (out of fear) comes with a heavy emotional price and often hinders people in the enjoyment of pursuing their goals. It should also be noted that being perfect in everything we do is unrealistic and quite often produces more feelings of guilt or shame than any positive emotions.

4) Feeling proud: Feeling overly proud of yourself once you have achieved your goals might also be an indication of a conditional view of self-esteem. Adopting an unconditional view of self-esteem means that if you cannot do certain things, if you failed in a certain goal, it should not affect your feelings about your self-worth. You might be sad about having failed in a certain goal, but it should not touch your core self-esteem. In the same way, this is the case for success in your goals. We can enjoy our achievements, but we should not feel that we are now a better person – again, our core self-esteem should not be affected by our success. There is a great saying that really brings this message home: all people are equal, but those who really understand this are somehow different.

5) Finally, a good example of unconditional love is also parental love: no matter what your child is doing, you still love them. You might have to correct their behaviour, but at the same time, you always convey unconditional love.

A great exercise that can help with increasing an unconditional view of our self-esteem is the following exercise by Kristin Neff (2020). It has three parts. The first is to reflect on yourself and recognise which imperfections make you feel inadequate. Everyone has things about themselves that they do not like because no human is perfect. Pick one issue and write about it and how it makes you feel. The second part of the exercise is to create an imaginary friend who loves you unconditionally. Think about what they feel about you, that they understand how your life circumstances have shaped you, and how they love you exactly as you are. Write a letter to yourself from them, focussing on the issue you identified in part one. How would they convey their compassion, explain that everyone has both strengths and weaknesses, and possibly give some advice? Most importantly, as Neff says, "As you write to yourself from the perspective of this imaginary friend, try to infuse your letter with a strong sense of his/her acceptance, kindness, caring, and desire for your health and happiness." Finally, part three of the exercise is to put the letter aside for a little while, then read it, feeling the compassion as you do.

However, admitting our flaws and imperfections is challenging, and owning them even more so. It can make one feel extremely vulnerable. Unfortunately, staying silent and trying to hide the negatives, or even remaining in denial about having them, creates a great sense of shame in ourselves: we are not good enough. This in turn fuels the conditional self-esteem. If we can swallow the fear and the shame and talk about our imperfections, their shaming power can disappear. It is hugely liberating when we reclaim our power, and this will lead to unconditional self-esteem.

One way that might help you to overcome that fear is to think about what vulnerability means. This is a great definition:

> Vulnerability is not winning or losing; it's having the courage to show up and be seen when we have no control over the outcome. Vulnerability is not weakness; it's our greatest measure of courage.
>
> (Brown, 2015, p. 4)

Another fact that may help is that self-disclosure through writing or talking can help relieve stress – research has demonstrated improvements to the immune system and less subsequent visits to the doctor (Pennebaker et al., 1988).

All these exercises and thoughts are about your general view of yourself and ways to help you adopt a more self-compassionate view towards yourself. But this book is all about thinking about your most important goals in life. So, the key is in applying this thinking around self-compassion to your most important goals.

Strategy 1: reduce goal-striving for ego reasons

The first thing to ask yourself is why these goals are so important to you and what you hope to get out of them. Then the crucial part is to analyse how much of your motivation is about your self-esteem or, in other words, your ego. How large is that part of your motivation that thinks you are more worthy than before once you have accomplished your goal, or, even more importantly, that you are worth less if you fail in this goal? If this part is noticeably big, then research would suggest you should stop striving for this goal for this particular reason. It does not get you where you want to be in the first place and once you have proven to yourself that you are worthy by achieving a particular goal, the next goal where your self-esteem is again "on the line" is just around the corner.

It is important to note here that sometimes it is not necessary to change the goal. Instead, you can still strive for the same goal, but do it for different reasons. This can then change the way you experience and enjoy the pursuit of this goal. To explain this, we will use a fictional scenario, though some aspects of it might feel familiar:

> John is working on a project for work. He is anxious because he is worried about not doing a good enough job. He knows that if he does not do well enough to get praise from his manager, it will reinforce his feelings that he is just not good enough and simply not capable of doing his job. He knows he will feel like a failure. The more he thinks about this, the more it becomes the singular thought driving him to try to succeed. John feels more anxious and starts to disengage from his work. He is definitely not enjoying striving for the goal of accomplishing this project.
>
> John then chides himself for trying to achieve this for the purpose of proving to himself that he is worthy. He reminds himself to be kind to himself and that he is doing the best job he can and should be happy with himself for that; that if he fails, it would not be because he was incapable, but instead because there were still unknown elements and that some aspects were beyond his control. He is then able to start thinking about the bigger picture. He becomes excited as he thinks about the benefits for others that could come from completion of this project. He loves the fact that he could have such a positive impact. This separation of the task and goal (the external situation) from himself as a person, helps John switch the reason for accomplishing his goal from one of self-esteem to one of helping others. This puts him in a positive mental space, enabling him to enjoy the pursuit of this goal. With a smile on his face, he re-engages in his work.

As we can see from our fictional scenario, the same goal can be pursued for different reasons and, to a large extent, those reasons determine how much people enjoy that pursuit. On top of this, different reasons can also lead to different actions and behaviours that can lead to different levels of productivity. For example, if trying to prove your self-esteem, you might engage in more self-promoting behaviours such as working long hours or only when the boss is around to be seen as hard working. The first can unnecessarily lead to exhaustion which will negatively impact the quality of the work (not

Table 6.1 Reflection on goal-striving reasons

What is my goal?	Why do I strive for it?	Is any part of this about me needing to feel more of a good/ worthy person?	If I fail in this goal, would I think of myself as not good enough/a failure?	Can I stop striving for this goal for this particular reason?	How do I do this? What do I need to stop doing?
Goal 1					
Goal 2					
Goal 3					
Goal 4					

to mention your health!). The second can mean that aspects of the work are not done at the optimal time for the tasks concerned, such as when needed colleagues are around, thus unnecessarily causing delays.

By reflecting on your goal-striving reasons and the subsequent behaviours that might ensue, you will be able to reframe your reasoning and change your behavioural responses. Table 6.1 can help.

Strategy 2: learning goals (and how to deal with failure)

Another great concept to apply to the idea of dealing with success and failure in a way that does not negatively impact our self-esteem is the concept of learning goals (Dweck & Leggett, 1988). Much like happiness, achieving a goal is a journey and your contributions along the way are important. It is not simply about the actions you take to achieve the goal, but also about what skills and capabilities you would need to improve to be able to work towards your goal. Rather than simply focusing on the outcome, by including a focus on your learning and development, the goal becomes a learning goal. It is this difference that has important implications for your emotional well-being, and therefore your happiness, when dealing with success and failure.

To illustrate the difference between the two, we will start with the outcome goal, also known as a performance goal. An example is marking the success of a project by generating a turnover of £100,000. Another example is obtaining a master's degree. These have a specific end point that must be reached for the goal to be considered successfully achieved. Outcome goals are the most typical type of goal that people pursue (Markman, 2014). So, what happens if you succeed in this project? On the one hand, you are obviously going to be happy about that. However, at the same time, you might not be as happy as you possibly could be. Why? Because all you have done is shown yourself that you are capable of doing what you thought you were capable of doing. You have confirmed what you already knew. On the other hand, if you fail in this goal, you have shown yourself that you are not as capable as you thought you were. This can consequently have a strong negative impact on your self-esteem.

Now let us take the performance goal of obtaining a master's degree and change it to a learning goal. Rather than simply focussing on the final outcome, you think carefully about the skills and capabilities you could improve that would make you a better student and possibly lead to a higher mark in your degree, for example, the speed with which you can read textbooks, your critical thinking skills, your literature research skills, your presentation skills, your note-taking skills in lectures, your academic writing skills, etc. Once you complete the goal, it is no longer just that you have achieved something that you thought you were able to achieve. It is now also that you have shown yourself that you have improved your skillset – that you have become better and grown as a person. If you attribute your success to these kinds of things, you will likely be even happier about your success than someone simply pursuing a performance goal. However, even more important is what happens when you fail in parts of your journey towards the degree. For example, you fail a module. In this case, it is not that you are not good enough. It is that you have not learned enough yet. "Yet" is a keyword here. Failure becomes a learning opportunity. As a result, it is far less self-esteem diminishing because you still feel you can achieve it; you just need to improve even more. Or perhaps you improved in one skill but then realised that there is another crucial skill that was necessary. Similarly, you might have failed because external circumstances have changed. Regardless, you will not feel as bad in this scenario because you have improved in a skill, and no one can take that away from you.

So, developing learning goals instead of performance goals is a powerful way to deal with failure and successes during goal pursuit – by which we mean a way that contributes the most to your happiness. Here is a little exercise (see Table 6.2) that can help with transforming any performance goals you might have into learning goals. For each goal, make a list of skills that would increase the likelihood of achieving that goal or that might help you get better results. Next, narrow down the list to the top three or four for each goal. The idea of only selecting up to four is that trying to improve more than this can make the process of achieving the goal too much work which could lead to giving up. The skills you select should be important to the goals, but also relevant to you – everyone's skill sets are different.

Table 6.2 Transforming performance goals into learning goals

Performance goal	Skill/capability 1 I want to become better at:	Skill/capability 2 I want to become better at:	Skill/capability 3 I want to become better at:	Skill/capability 4 I want to become better at:
Goal 1				
Goal 2				
Goal 3				
Goal 4				

References

Brown, B. (2015). *Rising strong*. London: Vermilion.

Crocker, J., & Knight, K. M. (2005). Contingencies of self-worth. *Current Directions in Psychological Science*, 14(4), 200–203. doi: 10.1111/j.0963-7214.2005.00364.x

Dweck, C. S., & Leggett, E. L. (1988). A social-cognitive approach to motivation and personality. *Psychological Review*, 95(2), 256–273. doi: 10.1037/0033-295X.95.2.256

Markman, A. (2014). *Smart change: Five tools to create new and sustainable habits in yourself and others*. New York: Penguin Group LLC.

Neff, K. D. (2020). *Exercise 3: Exploring self-compassion through writing*. Retrieved February 4, 2020, from https://self-compassion.org/exercise-3-exploring-self-compassion-writing/

Pennebaker, J. W., Kiecolt-Glaser, J. K., & Glaser, R. (1988). Disclosure of traumas and immune function: Health implications for psychotherapy. *Journal of Consulting and Clinical Psychology*, 56(2), 239–245. doi: 10.1037/0022-006X.56.2.239

Chapter 7

Pleasure

Important goals that you pursue because they are enjoyable

One of the happiness-increasing reasons for pursuing a goal is because we enjoy that pursuit. However, it is important to remember that we are talking about our most important goals in life and not just any goal or activity that simply gives us pleasure, such as a nice meal. It is rather that our most important goals – the things we want to achieve in life the most – should be pleasurable or enjoyable.

Strategy 1: match your goals with your heart

The idea of creating and pursuing highly enjoyable goals that will contribute to our happiness seems obvious. However, many people have difficulty in finding those goals or struggle to pursue their goals in such a way that they find enjoyable. Indeed, research has shown that people all too often pursue goals they do not enjoy. One reason for this is the fact that people at times find it difficult to recognise what they actually enjoy. In other words, they find it difficult to listen to their heart – to their emotions. To be able to listen to your emotions is a skill and, as with all skills, people differ in the degree to which they have acquired this skill. But emotions are a vital part of our existence and can greatly influence what we are doing. Unfortunately, all too often we give priority to the importance of the goal (the rational or logical side of goal setting) and feel we just have to achieve it no matter how much of a drag it is, instead of thinking about how to make it more enjoyable to pursue. Note that we are not suggesting changing the goal to anything less important. We are only talking about modifying the way we pursue our goal.

There is a whole body of research on the matching of one's goals to one's emotional needs. These needs are called implicit motives in the literature and are defined as relatively stable, unconscious needs (McClelland, 1980), representing affective preferences that evolve gradually through learning and experience (McClelland, 1985). In simple terms, implicit motives are our emotional needs and the reasons why we enjoy certain things in life. They are implicit as they do not stem from a conscious thinking process: we do not make a deliberate decision on what we will enjoy. It just happens that we enjoy doing certain things and not other things. Thus, the reason why we enjoy certain activities is that they satisfy our implicit (unconscious) motives.

The most important motives in this context are McClelland et al.'s (1953) Big Three: the achievement motive, the affiliative motive, and the power motive. The achievement motive, or achievement motivation, is characterised by a behaviour that involves "competition with a standard of excellence" (McClelland et al., 1953, as cited in Brunstein & Heckhausen, 2008, p. 137). Thus, the need for achievement is the desire to excel or to accomplish something in relation to a personal standard of excellence. In other words, it is the desire to prove to oneself (and to others) how good we really are in areas that matter to us. The affiliative motive

> refers to a class of social interactions that is mundane but fundamental, the goal of which is to seek contact with formerly unknown or little-known individuals and to maintain that contact in a manner that both parties experience as satisfying, stimulating, and enriching. The motive is activated whenever we come into contact and interact with unknown or little-known individuals.
>
> (Sokolowski & Heckhausen, 2008, p. 185)

Thus, the need for affiliation is a need for positive interpersonal relationships. The need for power is "the need primarily to feel strong, and secondarily to act powerfully. Influencing others is just one of several ways of satisfying the need to feel strong" (McClelland, 1975, as cited in Schmalt & Heckhausen, 2008, p. 204). Thus, the desire to have control over others and to be influential arises from the need for power.

In the context of all three motives (achievement, affiliation, and power), it is also important to note that one needs to further distinguish between an approach and avoidance component within each of the three categories of motives. For example, in addition to the tendency to prove to oneself how good we are (approach achievement motive; hope of success), there is also the tendency to be afraid to fail in this attempt (avoidance motive; fear of failure). In the same way that one might have the desire to exert power (hope of power) there is also the component of not having or losing power (fear of losing power). Equally, with the approach component of the affiliative motive (hope of affiliation), there is also an avoidance component (fear of rejection). This is important to consider as this obviously influences the kind of emotions we experience when we take on a challenge, for example. Here, depending on people's achievement motive, people might have very different experiences:

- High approach achievement motive: looking forward to and thriving on a challenge; feeling excitement

- High avoidance achievement motive: being afraid to fail in a challenge; feeling fear
- High approach **and** high avoidance achievement motive: both emotions at the same time
- Low achievement motive: a challenge is not appealing to this person; this is not something this person thrives on

Similar combinations (strong approach motive/low avoidance motive; low approach motive/strong avoidance motive; strong approach/strong avoidance; low approach/low avoidance) are possible for the power and affiliative motives.

It is important to note that you cannot consciously detect your implicit motives, so a different form of diagnosis is useful. Research has developed a few diagnostic tools with which one can "measure" one's implicit motive structure. The most famous are probably the thematic apperception test (TAT; Murray, 1943) and the multi-motive grid (MMG; Sokolowski et al., 2000). This book cannot offer these kinds of diagnostic tools. However, by using the conceptual framework on the three implicit motives (achievement, affiliative, and power) that we have provided as a guide, you can consider ideas on how to modify your goals so that you enjoy them more. Essentially, this is the ultimate test of whether you have applied the concept of matching your (explicit) goals with your implicit motives: you enjoy the pursuit of your goals more than before.

Thus, your knowledge about those three implicit motives (achievement, affiliation, and power) and how you think you score on them allows you to come up with some working hypotheses on ways you could modify your goals so as to enjoy them more. A very simple example of applying the knowledge to modify your goals would be if you think that you have a strong approaching social motive, then it would make sense to go for a run with others rather than doing it alone. You would still be working on the same goal (becoming fitter) but in such a way that you enjoy it more. You can also combine certain strategies with each other. Sticking with our running example, if you feel you have a strong achievement motive, you could take your running group to a running competition. This could force you to improve your running times for a certain distance which might give you an additional boost. Finally, if you also believe you have a high approaching power motive you could also organise the running group. Hopefully this example gives you an indication of how you can pursue your goals in such a way that you find them more enjoyable because the more you enjoy what you do, the greater the likelihood of achieving your goals!

Below are some general strategies to consider that might help you with modifying your goals in such a way that fit better with your implicit motives to make them (even) more enjoyable. When you do this though, always remember it is your emotions that decide if the changes you have made really helped you modify your goals in such a way that you now enjoy the pursuit of your goal more than before. If you think you applied the concept of matching your goals to your implicit motives correctly but do not enjoy your goals more than before, then there is something wrong. This could be because you have the wrong perception of your implicit motives, or perhaps you have not found the right modification to your goals.

Table 7.1 Matching goals to implicit motives

	Approach component	Avoidance component
Achievement motive	• Increase the size or number of challenges in goals • Make it competitive • Measure yourself	• Take smaller steps (less overwhelming) • Don't do everything at once; don't attempt to win or do battle • Just do things, don't measure • Share the challenge with others (do it together)
Affiliative (social) motive	• Do things with others, not alone	• Think about whether you would prefer doing things on your own • Approach unfamiliar people with close friends/family for support
Power motive	• Take responsibility • Take leadership roles • Be an informal leader • Try to help others • Try to influence people, try to get them onboard	• Choose easier situations (e.g., with kids rather than adults) • Give up responsibility; help and support others (be their wingman)

Additionally, there are a few strategies you can use to better access your implicit motives. The first one is to repeatedly clench and unclench your left fist, which will activate areas of the right brain. As implicit networks representing needs and preferences are located in the right side of the brain, this exercise is believed to facilitate awareness of implicit motives and core values, thus aiding awareness of one's compatibility with goal assignments and judgements of preferences (Baumann et al., 2005). The second strategy is to frequently monitor your bodily states. At regular intervals, take note of how you are feeling, e.g., hunger, fatigue, tense, bored, happy, etc. Research suggests that people who regularly practise this have higher awareness of and sensitivity to their internal states. This awareness can promote greater understanding of one's implicit motives, thus making them better at aligning their goals to their implicit motives (Thrash et al., 2007). In addition, behaving as consistently as possible, i.e., adopting a similar demeanour and expressing similar values across a diverse range of situations, has also been shown to foster this congruence (Thrash et al., 2007).

Another important consideration regarding matching one's goals to one's implicit motives (our emotional side) is how we deal with the extrinsic temptations thrown at us. For example, a friend of mine once told me about one of his relatives who is a firefighter and has been all his life. He was so good that he was offered a promotion to become the manager of the entire firefighting department in one of the biggest cities in Germany. As you can imagine, that would have been a big step up in terms of salary, status, etc. – many extrinsic rewards. But he declined the offer because of the following reason. He said, "My heart, my desire is really when I go out and help people in need and putting out fires. This is what I am all about." The question now for you reading this is what would you have done, and why? Where do your priorities lie?

Some might wonder if the extra money and status might equally increase their happiness and is thus worth sacrificing the part of the job that they love. Research suggests not. In analysing data from 40 nations, Diener and Oishi (2000) found that the correlation between income and subjective well-being was very small ($r = 0.13$). When this was broken down, people with lower incomes were found to be unhappier. However, whilst they seemed to benefit from a happiness boost with a rise in income, those with higher incomes did not. It seems that once basic living needs are met, income no longer has a corresponding rise in subjective well-being.

Strategy 2: do something fun – on a regular basis

In addition to the notion that it is generally a positive thing to enjoy the things we are doing, research has also shown that having positive emotions also has so-called "positive spill-over effects" for us. Fredrickson (2004) has studied this phenomenon which led to the development of the broaden-and-build theory. According to this theory, positive emotions cause us to be more creative and innovative, more resourceful, and more optimistic. Thus, positive emotions create a virtuous cycle: the positive emotions bring us into a state where we have the best ideas and where we feel the most resourceful when we think about how we want to pursue our goals.

The implications of this knowledge are again quite simple. Do something on a regular basis that you really enjoy. As simple as this may sound, many people struggle with it. Quite often, people find something which comes under the banner of, "Once I do it, I enjoy it, but I need to force myself to do it." But we can do one better than this: is there anything you really enjoy that you would not need to force yourself to do?

It is also important to think about the timing and variety of your fun activities. For example, imagine listening to your favourite song. What would happen if you listened to this song ten times a day for the next three weeks? You would probably lose interest in it and not enjoy it as much. Indeed, you might even get bored of it! So, the idea regarding timing is to think about the ideal period of time before repeating the activity. Perhaps once a week is a good interval and you only listen to your favourite song on a Monday to boost yourself up for the week. Is going for a swim every other day enough of a break or would you get more out of swim if you only went once a week?

They say variety is the spice of life! With this factor, you can listen to music every day. For example, you could have seven top songs, one for each day of the week for a daily boost. If you think of your activities as categories, then the possibilities are many. Rather than have a narrow focus such as swimming, expand it to the category of exercising. Then you could vary your activity by going for a bike ride, a run, doing a (virtual) physical education (PE) lesson, going to the gym, or doing some weights to tone your body. You could even create your own personal triathlon: go for a (shortish) run, then cycle to the local swimming pool and have a swim and then cycle home again – this would be great variety within the activity. It also works for other things such as reading a book. Here you could increase variety by reading two or three books at the same time on different subjects. Or you could read one book and listen to another audiobook. So, to put all this into practice, have a go at listing all the fun activities you can think of. Also, think about the period of repetition as well as the variety within the fun activity.

Table 7.2 Fun activities

Fun activity	How often do you want to repeat it to get the biggest happiness boost out of it?	Can you create some variety within the exercise?
Exercising	Three days in between each session	Run, cycle, lift weights, walk, swim

Another point to note is the fact that people all too often get caught up in day-to-day business and put the things they really enjoy on the backburner. Then, before they know it, half a year has passed without them having done anything. So, to an extent, this chapter also serves to encourage people to give themselves permission to fight for just two hours per week where they do something for themselves, not to be selfish, but to gain those benefits of subsequently becoming more resourceful, creative, etc. This will often also lead to being a better partner, parent, colleague, etc. Remember, we cannot pour from an empty cup.

Building on the broaden-and-build theory (pun intended), aside from enjoying the positive feeling after completing the highly enjoyable activity, also try to capture (or at least be more mindful) of the thoughts and ideas that you may generate during and after a positive activity. These are the thoughts that often give rise to the next great idea and shape your life for the better. To coin a phrase, ride this wave and try to catch the next one rather than letting this wave die down. You never know where life will take you.

Finally, there is one last point to consider in this context. The suggestions we have made so far are essentially all about additional activities for you to do. But please be mindful, sometimes all we need is rest and maybe instead of doing more activities, your fun activity could also be to relax, unwind, and recharge your batteries. Let's face it; this could be equally enjoyable!

References

Baumann, N., Kuhl, J., & Kazen, M. (2005). Left-hemispheric activation and self-infiltration: Testing a neuropsychological model of internalization. *Motivation and Emotion*, 29(3), 135–163. doi: 10.1007/s11031-005-9439-x

Brunstein, J. C., & Heckhausen, H. (2008). Achievement motivation. In J. Heckhausen, & H. Heckhausen (Eds.), *Motivation and action* (pp. 137–183). New York: Cambridge University Press.

Diener, E., & Oishi, S. (2000). Money and happiness: Income and subjective well-being across nations. In E. Diener, & E. M. Suh (Eds.), *Culture and subjective well-being* (pp. 185–218). Cambridge, MA: MIT Press.

Fredrickson, B. L. (2004). The broaden-and-build theory of positive emotions. *Philosophical Transactions of the Royal Society B*, 359(1449), 1367–1378. doi: 10.1098/rstb.2004.1512

McClelland, D. C. (1980). Motive dispositions: The merits of operant and respondent measures. In L. Wheeler (Ed.), *Review of personality and social psychology* (Vol. l, pp. 10–41). Beverly Hills, CA: SAGE.

McClelland, D. C. (1985). How motives, skills, and values determine what people do. *American Psychologist*, 40(7), 812–825. doi: 10.1037/0003-066X.40.7.812

McClelland, D. C., Atkinson, J. W., Clark, R. A., & Lowell, E. L. (1953). *Century psychology series. The achievement motive*. New York, NY: Appleton-Century-Crofts. doi: 10.1037/11144-000

Murray, H. A. (1943). *Thematic apperception test*. Cambridge, MA: Harvard University Press.

Schmalt, H.-D., & Heckhausen, H. (2008). Power motivation. In J. Heckhausen, & H. Heckhausen (Eds.), *Motivation and action* (pp. 202–226). New York: Cambridge University Press.

Sokolowski, K., & Heckhausen, H. (2008). Social bonding: Affiliation motivation and intimacy motivation. In J. Heckhausen, & H. Heckhausen (Eds.), *Motivation and action* (pp. 184–201). New York: Cambridge University Press.

Sokolowski, K., Schmalt, H.-D., Langens, T. A., & Puca, R. M. (2000). Assessing achievement, affiliation, and power motives all at once: The Multi-Motive Grid (MMG). *Journal of Personality Assessment*, 74(1), 126–145. doi: 10.1207/S15327752JPA740109

Thrash, T. M., Elliot, A. J., & Schultheiss, O. C. (2007). Methodological and dispositional predictors of congruence between implicit and explicit need for achievement. *Personality and Social Psychology Bulletin*, 33(7), 961–974. doi: 10.1177/0146167207301018

Chapter 8

Altruism

Goals that make the world a better place

Another important driver of our goals is that through our own actions we could aim to help others. There is a substantial amount of research now showing that helping others makes us feel better about ourselves. The expression "the helper's high" is a great one in this context.

In an experiment that really highlights the power of helping others for your own happiness, Dunn et al. (2008) asked a group of people to rate their happiness in the morning. They were then given either $5 or $20, with half instructed to spend it on themselves while the other half told to spend the money on someone else. At the end of the day, the participants were once again asked to rate their happiness. Those who spent the money on others were significantly happier than those who spent it on themselves. However, somewhat surprisingly, the amount made no difference to levels of happiness! Thus, it seems that it is purely the act of giving that makes people happy rather than the amount of spending.

Interestingly, people do not seem to realise this benefit to their happiness exists. When another group were asked which condition would make them the happiest, they wrongly forecasted that spending on themselves would make them happier than spending on others, and the $20 would make them happier than the $5 (Dunn et al., 2008). Yes, there is always a chance that spending on others will not work for you, but isn't it worth a try?

Helping others is labelled as "acts of kindness" in the research literature. One of the leading happiness researchers, Sonja Lyubomirsky (2007), has conducted some interesting studies which clearly inform us on how to go about being kind to others for the most benefit. Beyond the obvious findings that performing acts of kindness can make you happier, the timing and variety is important – as you repeatedly perform the same act of kindness, the positive effects will start to diminish. It works the same way as with pleasurable, fun activities. As discussed in the previous chapter, if you listened to your favourite song over and over again you would at some point become bored of it. Things need to be mixed up with a variety of activities and an appropriate amount of time between the acts of kindness to get the biggest happiness boost. Performing acts of kindness also comes with a bonus effect for the future. A new study suggests that simply remembering past acts of kindness contributes to our happiness: "Our results suggest that happiness seekers and well-being interventionists consider recalling acts of kindness as a cost-effective practice to raise well-being" (Ko et al., 2019, p. 1).

So, now knowing that helping others is vital for our own happiness, how can you use this information to modify your goals? Below are some strategies you could use.

Strategy 1: engage in acts of kindness on a regular basis

One obvious strategy is to simply have a goal of performing acts of kindness regularly. To ensure sufficient variety, you would need to draw from a wide list of potential acts of kindness. Below is a comprehensive list of ideas (see Table 8.1; modified from The Sunshine People, 2020). Although all items may not apply to everyone, it does nonetheless present some great ideas and may inspire you to come up with more ideas of your own.

While creating your own list of acts of kindness is important, experience through teaching our Happiness Through Goal Setting course has shown us that people are very keen to have a list as long as humanly possible. However, more important than a long list is to come up with those acts of kindness that really speak to you, that really touch your heart. For example, the act of kindness to buy a second coffee at a coffee shop and ask for this coffee to be given to the next person is a great idea, especially if it is anonymous and they get their free coffee after you are long gone. However, relating back to the point we made about "it needs to matter to you", this particular act of kindness was never one that really worked for me. This is probably because I always felt the next person could be a millionaire and would be the last person who needs something for free. Therefore, the impact of this particular act of kindness felt a bit hit and miss. Having said that, it might be one that you find appealing. Regardless, the two key things are to have a list long enough for sufficient variety, and ensure they matter to you.

Finally, there is one last point to make here. Incorporating acts of kindness into your daily life is most successful when you do them spontaneously – when an opportunity presents itself. We are all busy people and do not necessarily have enough time to try to carefully plan and execute acts of kindness. However, seizing the moments as they occur is a helpful strategy. For example, picking up plastic waste on your way to work is easier to do than making time to go out for a walk specifically to pick up plastic. Being out for a meal presents the opportunity to have your leftovers packed in a doggy bag so that you can give them to a homeless person, should you

Table 8.1 Acts of Kindness ideas (modified from The Sunshine People, 2020)

Leave money in a vending machine for someone	Water a neighbour's lawn/flowers	Pay for someone's bus fare
Bake cookies for the elderly	Offer to take a photo for a couple	Offer someone your pen
Serve at a homeless shelter	Give someone a gift card that you don't intend to use	Lend a friend a favourite book
Do a 5k for a good cause		Recommend someone your favourite book/movie
Help at a veterinarian office	Wash someone's car	Take your younger siblings out to play in the rain
Pick up litter on the beach	Read to children at the library for story time	Make hot chocolate for your family on a cold day
Let someone go in front of you in a queue	Plan a surprise birthday party for someone	Take the time to appreciate the sunrise and sunset
Give a stranger a compliment	Perform a concert at a retirement home	Write someone an encouraging poem
Make dinner for a family in need	Help do chores at a farm/harvest ranch	Send colouring books to sick children in the hospital
Insert coins into someone's parking meter	Leave your waiter a generous tip	Celebrate your own best friend appreciation day
Buy flowers to hand out on the street	Start mentoring a younger child	Help tutor a struggling student
Leave letters of encourage-ment on people's cars	Spend time with your grandparents	Pay for another student's lunch
Donate your old clothes to a charity shop	Make a family member breakfast in bed	Offer to give a friend a ride home
Help a senior with their groceries	Hold the elevator for someone	Take the time to listen to someone
Shovel a neighbour's driveway when it snows	Pay for someone's dry cleaning	Recycle things that you see on the road
Walk a neighbour's dog	Pack someone a lunch for the day	Help sick animals find homes
Babysit for free	Write a kind or encouraging message on a napkin	Make someone a homemade blanket or scarf
Plant a tree	Do a sibling's chores without them asking	Feed the birds in the park
Do a favour without asking for anything in return	Offer to take a shopper's cart to the line outside	Leave some change on a wishing fountain
Take someone new in your neighbourhood on a tour of the city	Help someone who has a flat tire	Help out the janitors at school
Show the new kids around your school or work	Let someone else pick what to watch on TV	Donate your hair after a haircut
Buy an ice-cream cone for a child	Send care packages to soldiers overseas	Give your umbrella to a stranger
Learn to say hello in a different language to different people	Rake the leaves for your neighbours	Volunteer to work some overtime at your job
Prepare a meal for your family	Mow the lawn for your neighbours	Ride your bike or walk to work
Pay for a stranger's library fees	Take the day not to complain	Offer compliments to strangers and friends and family
Send Valentine's day cards to everyone in your class	Write a list of things that you adore about a friend	Buy your waiter/waitress dessert
Spend a day at a homeless shelter	Pay for someone's morning coffee	Wash a neighbour's dog for free
Give drinks out to people on a hot day	Instead of posting negativity online, spread some encouragement	Buy groceries for the person behind you
Send a letter to a good friend instead of a text	Share your favourite quote and post them to the company billboard	Reconnect with old friends
Bring in donuts for your co-workers		Hide money in random places for strangers to find
Help a child or older person cross the street	Give up your seat on the bus to another person	Be kind to yourself!

happen to pass one on your way home. Seeing someone's grocery bag break presents a great opportunity to stop and help them pick up their shopping. Noticing someone more in need of a seat than you get on the bus offers the opportunity to give up yours.

Strategy 2: reflect on your own impact

A simple way to build helping others into our goals is by becoming more sensitive to the impact our actions/goals have on others. Sometimes we are not completely aware, or we may even be unaware, of our positive impact on others. How intensively have you been thinking so far about what your positive impact is on others through your goals? Remember, even the little things matter.

There is a great exercise that can really help us become aware of the positive effects we have on others through our goals. It is called job crafting. It is through job crafting that we can always see our actions as part of a bigger picture. There are two ways to describe what you are doing: you can either describe the simple and actual action you are doing or you put your action in a bigger, and therefore more important, context. It is this bigger context that helps us to become aware that we are contributing to something greater than ourselves. There are two stories that explain this concept well. The first is about two stonemasons who are asked what they are doing. One (the non-job crafter) replies: I am cutting stones. The other stonemason illustrates job crafting beautifully with his response: I am helping to build a cathedral. Similarly, the other story is about a cleaner at NASA. When asked what his job was about, he replied: I am helping to bring people to the moon. Can you do this same exercise for yourself using Table 8.2?

Table 8.2 Your impact on others

What are your most important goals?	What are the wider implications of your actions for others, the community, society, the environment?
Goal 1	
Goal 2	
Goal 3	
Goal 4	

References

Dunn, E., Aknin, L., & Norton, M. I. (2008). Spending money on others promotes happiness. *Science, 319*(5870), 1687–1688. doi: 10.1126/science.1150952

Ko, K., Margolis, S., Revord, J., & Lyubomirsky, S. (2019). Comparing the effects of performing and recalling acts of kindness. *The Journal of Positive Psychology, 16*(1), 1–9. doi: 10.1080/17439760.2019.1663252

Lyubomirsky, S. (2007). *The how of happiness: A scientific approach to getting the life you want.* New York: Penguin Press.

The Sunshine People. (2020). *Kindness ideas.* Retrieved August 20, 2020, from https://www.sunshinepeople.org.uk/act-of-kindess-ideas

Chapter 9

Necessity

Goals that you pursue because you need to make a living

The last reason that affects our happiness is the degree to which we pursue a goal out of necessity. By that, we mean, are we striving for our goal because we feel we must do it to make a living? As we saw earlier, happiness does increase with income up to the point of meeting basic needs.

However, and particularly in the developed world, people inherently have difficulty in determining what is "necessary." Doing things out of the necessity to survive is quite often not the issue. The vast majority of people (though admittedly not everyone) have shelter, food, a car, and go on holiday at least once a year and are therefore, overall, reasonably well off. However, as humans, we quite often feel we need additional things to "survive." For example:

- We work hard so feel the need for more holidays
- The family is getting in each other's hair, so a bigger house is needed
- We must have a certain brand of car which might be excessively more expensive than an average car

There is nothing wrong with having this kind of luxury, but if you need to work even harder to be able to afford all these things, then you start to suffer in your day-to-day life. If the goals you strive for come with too much stress and anxiety, then it might be worthwhile considering whether they really are necessary.

It is also worthwhile reflecting on the level to which we feel the need to pursue goals out of necessity because research data strongly suggests that once we have our psychological needs met, then any additional material wealth doesn't seem to increase happiness levels by much (Diener & Biswas-Diener, 2002).

> Compared with their grandparents, today's young adults have grown up with much more affluence, slightly less happiness, and much greater risk of depression and assorted social pathologies ... Our becoming much

better off over the last four decades has not been accompanied by one iota of increased subjective well-being.

(Myers, 2000, p. 61)

There is a substantial body of literature that conclusively shows that materialism is not conducive for our happiness (beyond meeting our basic needs). For example, people with greater aspirations for financial success have lower levels of well-being and mental health (Kasser & Ryan, 1993; 1996). Nickerson et al. (2003) followed this up with a longitudinal study demonstrating the perpetuating effects of this phenomenon. They tracked students for 20 years and found consistent results in that those with stronger goals for financial success had correspondingly lower levels of life satisfaction, regardless of income. Overall, many studies confirm that the more people endorse materialistic goals, the less happy and satisfied they are with life (Belk, 1985; Kasser & Ryan, 1993; 1996; Richins & Dawson, 1992; Van Boven, 2005).

The issue we have as humans is that, materialistically, there will always be something else to strive for. When is enough enough? At what point do we stop and say, "I have enough"? Diener and Oishi (2000, p. 211) sum up this idea nicely, saying, "a more prosperous material world will not inevitably increase life satisfaction. If people's desires outstrip reality, it is likely that people would be more dissatisfied even in a very affluent world." The solution is not easy, though. As mentioned in Chapter 3, we seem to be genetically programmed to continually want more stuff as a now-obsolete method of survival.

Marketing makes it difficult for us too, as it taps into that psyche, propagating the belief that things are necessary. They manage to convince us that we will be better off in some manner, instilling a desire/want in us, and we willingly believe at some point that we must have the thing in question.

So, are there any possibilities that we can stop this and be less forced into wanting more? Is it possible to press the pause button and think about what we really need and want? Thankfully, the answer is yes. There are a few strategies we can harness to reset our brains and counter our impulses.

The minimalism movement is a useful philosophy for many. The core idea is to only keep those things that add something to your life and declutter yourself from everything else. For example, a simple question is, how many jumpers do you have and how many do you really need? To elaborate, do you like all of them and do you use all of them? Marie Kondo, a famous tidying expert with her KonMari method of decluttering, helped this concept trend with her simple question of, "Does this spark joy?" (Kondo, 2014, p. 47). If any item in your house is not contributing to your life, it should be given away and not replaced.

Anytime we are thinking about buying something new, it is well worth having a rummage around in the wardrobe first. For example, you might find that you actually do not need a new pair of jeans as there are two old, long-forgotten pairs in the back of the wardrobe.

Another idea is to think about the environment and be more considerate of our natural resources, so constantly buying new things, such as a new jumper, a new car, or the latest phone or flat-screen TV, is not helpful in this respect. As David Attenborough says in *Blue Planet* (2001), "Surely we all have a responsibility to care for our Blue Planet. The future of humanity and indeed, all life on earth, now depends on us." There are many people, researchers, activists, etc., that claim that we need to change our perception of success in life. It cannot be about the accumulation of material things – our world and our lives would be far better if it were about psychological wealth. Indeed, happiness does seem to be correlated with a value system in this vein. While the pursuit of extrinsic factors (financial success, an appealing appearance, and social recognition) is associated with lower levels of well-being, the greater value of intrinsic factors (self-acceptance, affiliation, community feeling, and physical health) has been found to be associated with greater well-being and less distress (Kasser & Ryan, 1996).

Strategy 1: how to avoid doing things out of necessity for your most important goals

A lot about reducing the need to gain material wealth is about reflection and making conscious choices. Ask yourself, is there an element of wanting more within the reasons why I want to achieve my goals? Maybe this is a starting point, knowing what the research says about this and deciding consciously not to fall into this trap – of wanting more – just for the sake of wanting more.

This might lead to the following: an agreement with yourself on what and how much you really need. This then leads to recognition of the saturation point – the point at which you do not need more. Charting what you need in Table 9.1 may help with this. As an example, if you come to the conclusion that you don't need that much money, this might mean that you could change your full-time job to part time and start up some side business/project you really enjoy. How could that change your life?

Strategy 2: reducing social comparison as another reason for why we want more

Sometimes the reason why we want more is not whether we have enough or not, but that we have less than others. Once we start comparing ourselves with others, it can lead to a downward spiral. If the comparison is negative, then we feel dissatisfied, less successful, and even resentful. This resentment that comes from feeling relatively deprived has been shown to increase materialism, making us feel we need more (Kim et al., 2017). This phenomenon, colloquially known as "keeping up with the Jones'", is researched under the label of social comparison theory (Festinger, 1954). This theory states

Table 9.1 What do you really need?

Item	How many/how big/how much?	Does it change the way I pursue my goals?
Car		
House		
Monthly Salary		

that we are driven to self-evaluate and we determine our social and personal worth based on how we stack up against others. As a result, we are constantly tempted to make self-evaluations and other-evaluations through upward and downward comparisons – who is better and who is worse – across a variety of domains (for example, attractiveness, wealth, intelligence, and success).

A common situation where this effect is found is on Facebook. People rarely post about the mundane, banal events of their lives. Posts tend to be of the high points, illustrating the amazing lives everyone is having. Unfortunately, the availability heuristic in our brains automatically kicks in and, not seeing their everyday stuff, leads us to believe that other people's lives are much better than our own. A weeklong experiment on 1,095 participants clearly demonstrated that taking a break from Facebook elevated two elements of well-being compared to those who did not take a break: life satisfaction increased and emotions became more positive (Tromholt, 2016).

Studies have also shown that social comparison is such a strong psychological force that sometimes we will choose to have less for ourselves if that means we are better off than others. For example, Van Boven (2005) conducted a study in which participants were asked to choose between the following two scenarios: they could either chose a yearly income of $50,000 while others earned $25,000 or a yearly income of $100,000 while others earned $200,000. Note that in the second scenario, participants would earn twice as much as they would in the first, but they would be worse off than others. Approximately half of the respondents reported that they would prefer the "positional outcome", in which they preferred to earn twice as much as their peers but less absolute money. Interestingly, different results were obtained in a little twist of Van Boven's research design where the scenarios were instead based on the length of holidays. Participants could choose to either have two weeks of holidays annually while others had only one week, or they could choose to have four weeks of holidays while others had eight weeks. Under this condition, only 15% of the respondents chose to have fewer holidays. Thus, unlike the results involving salary, most of the respondents (85%) would rather have longer holidays, even if their co-workers were to have a holiday twice as long. Van Boven explains this with the fact that experiences (i.e., holidays) are resistant to status concerns and therefore are more resistant to disadvantageous social comparisons.

One story that really brings this message home is the following fable (source unknown):

> There were two men living in a little village. One man was very conscientious – he always went to church and lived a very righteous life. However, he was not popular in the village. Whereas the second man, he was more of a jack of all trades, happy go lucky, and did not attend church, yet he was liked by everyone. One day the conscientious, hardworking man went to god and complained about the fact that, although he was living an honourable life no one really liked him, whereas the other man simply lived through the day but was liked by everyone. This is not fair, he said. God thought about this and understood the man's perspective, and so made him the following offer: I can see your predicament and I want to help you. I will grant you one wish. But beware, whatever you wish for, the other man will get twice as much of it. The man thought long and hard and then wished for the following: Make me blind in one eye.

Research has shown that happier people tend to engage in social comparison less. For example, in a study where people had to decide whether they would prefer to spend time with a happy friend who performed better than them or an unhappy, worse-performing friend, happy people preferred to spend time with the happy, superior friend (Kim et al., 2016). This suggests that happy people are less influenced by social comparison when deciding whom to spend time with and less likely to be deterred from being around people who might seem better than them. On the contrary, they reap the benefits of good company and the fact that they can learn from people who are better than themselves. This also fits with findings from Lyubomirsky and Ross (1997), who, based on two experimental studies with students, concluded that happy people tend to be less responsive to potentially negative social comparison information than unhappy people. In this context, the following oft-cited quote attributed to Maryam Hasnaa is particularly fitting, "Confidence isn't thinking you are better than everyone else, it's realising that you have no reason to compare yourself to anyone else."

So, knowing that social comparison is not helpful with regard to our own goals and our own happiness, the question arises of how we can reduce the tendency to compare ourselves with others. Given that the focus of this book is on our goals, it also raises the question as to how we can change our goals if we find that a strong driver behind our goals is the desire to be better than others.

Use more internal standards to evaluate your own progress rather than how you stack up in comparison with others

One strategy to reduce the amount of (external) social comparison we make is to focus more on an internal comparison, i.e., to compare myself with myself (Lyubomirsky & Ross, 1997). This means using our own standards of where we want to be rather than where we are compared to others. A common example is runners wanting to continually improve their best time or weightlifters wanting to increase the amount they are lifting. They will tend to focus on personal bests more than being better than others while training. The real trick is to transfer this into a competitive situation. Marathon runners will often talk about trying to improve their own time with each marathon they run, rather than focusing on how many other people they beat. Frank Dick was the British Athletics Federation's director of coaching and widely acknowledged as one of the best coaches in the world. He has trained many athletes to glory through this philosophy, "Winning is being better today than you were yesterday" (Dick, 2016). He illustrates his philosophy with an example of a little girl he trained. After a few weeks of training, she had her first race. She came last and was extremely disappointed. Frank, on the other hand, told her how well she had done by running her personal best in this race, giving her a very different perspective on the meaning of winning: winning is improving yourself, rather than being better or worse than others.

Such a strategy can work with many different aspects of life. For example, rather than wanting to buy a house as big as your friend's, focus on buying a house with one more room than you currently have for some specific purpose or a smaller house in a perfect location for your needs. Instead of needing to weigh less than your friend, ditch the scales and just lose weight until you like what you see in the mirror. Instead of competing with your colleague at work as to who can look better in their manager's eyes by making more sales or completing more projects, focus on comparing your current sales to your own previous levels, or finding the projects you are most passionate about to really make a difference.

Interestingly, this idea of creating an internal standard rather than an external standard is very much in line with the notion of setting oneself learning goals (see Chapter 6). For example, Lyubomirsky and Ross (1997,

p. 1153) state in this context, "happy individuals may be more inclined than unhappy ones to view their abilities as malleable rather than fixed", which, according to Latham (2012), means that they are more likely to set themselves learning goals rather than performance goals. Learning goals would therefore seem to be an ideal way to prevent social comparison and focus on your own development.

Make it a goal to be okay with people who are better than you

From a goal perspective, another way of "combatting" social comparison could be to simply make this in itself a new goal of yours. Try to learn to "be okay" with the fact that other people are better than you in certain things. Their success is not your failure! You could even go one step further and actually celebrate and enjoy the fact that you can live with or indeed accept the fact that other people are better than you, have a bigger house, or whatever it is. Remember that everyone is an individual with different abilities, circumstances, and needs. Celebrate this difference instead of trying to match it. Also, be mindful of where your focus lies. Are you wistfully thinking about what they have, or are you finding contentment with what you have? Imagine the feeling you could get from not having any negative emotions whatsoever at watching someone be better than you. Would that not be a fantastic feeling to have? It is possible. Be happy for them, and perhaps even learn from them, thus gaining something else in the process too.

Remind yourself that nobody has it all

With regards to avoiding social comparison, it might also be helpful to remember that nobody has it all. We seem to always compare the worst of what we know about ourselves to the best assumptions we make about others. That is why we need to remind ourselves that nobody has it all. Every person you meet experiences problems, trials, and weaknesses, just like you. This is what makes us human. Nobody is exempt, nobody has it all, and there is no such thing as perfect, "The very definition of being 'human' means that one is mortal, vulnerable and imperfect" (Neff, 2008, p. 5).

Unfortunately, the tendency to believe that some people have it all is caused by a strong psychological effect called the halo effect. Humans are quick in forming first impressions. Very often, these are based on only one or two things, such as appearance or behaviour. Those impressions, whether positive or negative, then create a halo around that person, leading to assumptions of an overall positive or negative impression, respectively. (A negative halo effect is also known as a horn effect.) The halo effect makes it possible to assume someone who is attractive is a good leader. It can lead to assumptions about a person's work ethic based on how formally they dress

Table 9.2 Reducing social comparison

Who are the people you feel are better than you in a particular aspect that matters to you?	Can you focus more on internal comparison?	Can you start celebrating the fact that you have learned/grown to accept that they are better?	Are there any aspects with which you think the other person is struggling (avoiding the halo effect)?

in the workplace. A company may try to use the halo effect to increase brand loyalty by creating good impressions of their green policies, despite their products not being particularly good quality. A colleague that you know to not work as hard as you may get promoted above you because of the manager's perceived halo effect based on some unrelated trait or behaviour in the past. A family living in an amazing house can trigger the thought that family life must be harmonious, and everyone is happy. What does not cross one's mind is that this family will likely also have conflicts and that these parents probably struggle with their kids just like any other family in the world.

So, to know that we as human beings have such a tendency to preclude from one positive aspect that someone is "perfect" in all ways might be a good starting point to avoid feeling bad about yourself or even inferior. The halo effect is a cognitive bias – it is a mechanism within us that shifts our perception of things away from reality. With a conscious realisation of this fact, we can avoid being conned by the halo effect.

So, the arguments presented about internal comparison, accepting (or indeed celebrating) that others are better than us, and the notion that no one has it all (halo effect) all lead to the exercise below, which you might find useful.

References

Attenborough, D. (2001). *The blue planet* [Television Series]. London, UK: BBC.
Belk, R. W. (1985). Materialism: Trait aspects of living in the material world. *Journal of Consumer Research*, 12(3), 265–280. doi: 10.1086/208515

Dick, F. (2016). *What is winning?* Retrieved August 11, 2020, from https://www.youtube.com/watch?v=wIrdZ9PWahc

Diener, E., & Biswas-Diener, R. (2002). Will money increase subjective well-being? *Social Indicators Research, 57,* 119–169.

Diener, E., & Oishi, S. (2000). Money and happiness: Income and subjective well-being across nations. In E. Diener, & E. M. Suh (Eds.), *Culture and subjective well-being* (pp. 185–218). Cambridge, MA: MIT Press.

Festinger, L. (1954). A theory of social comparison processes. *Human Relations, 7*(2), 117–140. doi: 10.1177/001872675400700202

Kasser, T., & Ryan, R. M. (1993). A dark side of the American dream: Correlates of financial success as a central life aspiration. *Journal of Personality and Social Psychology, 65*(2), 410–422. doi: 10.1037/0022-3514.65.2.410

Kasser, T., & Ryan, R. M. (1996). Further examining the American dream: Differential correlates of intrinsic and extrinsic goals. *Personality and Social Psychology Bulletin, 22*(3), 280–287. doi: 10.1177/0146167296223006

Kim, H., Callan, M. J., Gheorghiu, A. I., & Matthews, W. J. (2017). Social comparison, personal relative deprivation, and materialism. *British Journal of Social Psychology, 56*(2), 373–392. doi: 10.1111/bjso.12176

Kim, J., Hong, E. K., Choi, I., & Hicks, J. A. (2016). Companion versus comparison: Examining seeking social companionship or social comparison as characteristics that differentiate happy and unhappy people. *Personality and Social Psychology Bulletin, 42*(3), 311–322. DOI: 10.1177/0146167216629120

Kondo, M. (2014). *The life-changing magic of tidying: A simple, effective way to banish clutter forever.* London: Vermilion.

Latham, G. P. (2012). *Work motivation. History, theory, research, and practice* (2nd ed.). Los Angeles, CA: Sage Publications.

Lyubomirsky, S., & Ross, L. (1997). Hedonic consequences of social comparison: A contrast of happy and unhappy people. *Journal of Personality and Social Psychology, 73*(6), 1141–57. doi: 10.1037//0022-3514.73.6.1141

Myers, D. G. (2000). The funds, friends, and faith of happy people. *American Psychologist, 55*(1), 56–67. DOI: 10.1037//0003-066X.55,1.56

Neff, K. D. (2008). Self-compassion: Moving beyond the pitfalls of a separate self-concept. In J. Bauer, & H. A. Wayment (Eds.) *Transcending self-interest: Psychological explorations of the quiet ego* (pp. 95–105). Washington, DC: APA Books.

Nickerson, C., Schwarz, N., Diener, E., & Kahneman, D. (2003). Zeroing on the dark side of the American dream: A closer look at the negative consequences of the goal for financial success. *Psychology Science, 14*(6), 531–536. doi: 10.1046/j.0956-7976.2003.psci_1461.x.

Richins, M. L., & Dawson, S. (1992). A consumer values orientation for materialism and its measurement: Scale development and validation. *Journal of Consumer Research, 19*(3), 303–316. doi: 10.1086/209304

Tromholt, M. (2016). The Facebook experiment: Quitting Facebook leads to higher levels of well-being. *Cyberpsychology, Behaviour and Social Networking, 19*(11), 661–666. doi: 10.1089/cyber.2016.0259

Van Boven, L. (2005). Experientialism, materialism, and the pursuit of happiness. *Review of General Psychology, 9*(2), 132–142. doi: 10.1037/1089-2680.9.2.132

Part 3

Related topics around goals

Chapter 10

Assertiveness and assertiveness techniques

The next two chapters cover two related areas that can help with modifying your goals in such a way as to make them more enjoyable, more altruistic, less ego-driven, and less out of necessity. The first area is assertiveness and the second is creativity.

If you want to pursue goals that you really enjoy, then we believe you need to pursue your goals in your own way and shape your goals according to what you want. However, you are not pursuing your goals in isolation from others. Moreover, others might have certain expectations about you and your behaviour, which may even "force" you to behave in a certain way. The way we want to pursue our goals or, indeed, the kind of goals we want to pursue is not always handed to us on a plate. This means that at times we need to assert ourselves in a way that ensures that we can do the things we want in the way we want. In other words, we have to be assertive and "fight for our goals".

It should be noted here that when we say "fight", we are not talking about being aggressive and violating the rights of others. The difference between being assertive and being aggressive is a common source of confusion and is an important distinction that needs to be explained. Imagine a spectrum in the form of a line (see Figure 10.1): passive lies at one end, and aggressive lies at the other. Many people are polite, caring, and considerate of others to the detriment of themselves. It is a common belief that when we care about others, we should sacrifice ourselves and what we need to ensure they are happy. This is being passive regarding your own needs. It is a lose-win scenario where you lose (suffer/do not get what you need) and the other person wins, often oblivious to any sacrifice on your part. On the other end of our spectrum is being aggressive. Relatively self-explanatory, this one is a win-lose scenario where you win, and the other person loses.

In the middle lies the hallowed middle ground of assertiveness. It is here that we can find the optimal solution that works for all parties involved: the win-win scenario. Sometimes we cannot find the ultimate solution and so may end up with a compromising solution where each party sacrifices a little but wins a little to meet in the middle. Regardless, being assertive means

Figure 10.1 What is assertiveness?

that everything is done in a considered and respectful way and no one suffers unduly. And remember that you can be a good, kind person and still say no.

Returning to the context of pursuing our goals, assertiveness should serve two functions: either to fight for activities or things we want to do more of within our goals or to fight to get rid of things we do not want to do anymore or at least want to do less of. There is now some empirical evidence showing that the quality of goal-reasons is correlated with people's overall assertiveness levels (Ehrlich, 2018; 2019). As such, because the reasons why we do things can be strongly influenced by others, it is therefore important to harness some level of assertiveness to ensure we are doing things for the right reasons.

Here we focus on three popular and well-established techniques – all of which are particularly suitable when it comes to negotiations in relation to your goals. They are I-statements, reciprocity and concessions, and the broken record.

I-statements

I-statements are a great way to express what you want but in a respectful way! They are used to voice one's feelings and wishes from a personal position without putting blame or judgement on the other person. It is never guaranteed that you will get what you want, but this is a powerful technique with which to try. Many times, people censor themselves and do not express their wishes. There are various reasons as to why this might be the case: perhaps because they think they would never get what they want anyway, it may be because they don't want to be a bother or nuisance, or maybe they are afraid of upsetting or offending others. But people are not mindreaders, and letting others know what you want is a necessary starting point. An extremely easy way of checking how much you hold yourself back is the following exercise:

> Over the course of a whole day, make a note of every time you did not say something despite having an initial urge to do so or feeling that something was not quite right. How many times did this happen? Why did each occurrence happen? Was it for one of the reasons mentioned above? Perhaps you genuinely thought it was not worthwhile for some other reason. Regardless, if you noticed that this happened more than you expected or liked, then this chapter on assertiveness is for you. Also, keep in mind that the act of becoming more assertive is a great opportunity for another learning goal.

I-statements are an ideal method of finding a way to voice your feelings and make requests. An I-statement ultimately has the following parts. They start with you stating the specific behaviour of the other person. They continue by explaining what that behaviour does to you in terms of how this behaviour makes you feel. Again, you need to be specific. For example, rather than simply saying I am sad or angry, explain with more specifics: I am angry because when you talk to me like that, I feel disrespected or not taken seriously. The third thing to tell the other person is the impact their behaviour has on you (e.g., I fear that this is hurting our relationship; I am becoming more disconnected from you). Keep in mind you need to say all three things to make an I-statement effective. If you drop one of the three elements, it will not work as well, or possibly not at all. If the person comes back to you with a counterargument, just repeat your I-statement (see the section below on the broken record technique). Eventually, the other person will start taking responsibility for their actions. The most important reason why I-statements work is that they are different from you-statements where you blame the other person and tell them that they are the problem. Instead of the focus being on them, the focus is on you and how things affect or impact you. A good, though not essential, way to close an I-statement is to state what you would prefer to happen – your request as it were.

Here are some examples:

Table 10.1 Changing you-statements into I-statements

You-statement	I-statement
Stop interrupting me!	I feel frustrated when I am interrupted, it makes me lose my train of thought. I would prefer it if you let me finish my sentences before saying something.
You're late again!	I feel frustrated when you come late to our meetings. I don't like having to repeat information.
Stop micromanaging me!	I feel frustrated when you micromanage me and tell me how to do every little thing in my job. I would prefer it if you told me the main tasks that need to be done and then let me figure out what the best way for me is to accomplish them.
I can't believe you ruined my jacket!	I feel really upset because you have ruined my jacket, and I am starting to question whether I can lend you some of my precious things in the future.
Why will you not let me work from home on a Friday? I could work more effectively.	Not allowing me to work from home on Fridays makes me feel that I am not trusted enough as an employee, and this is causing me to be less enthusiastic about my workplace. I am also not as effective as I could be in the noisy work environment.

Another reason to use I-statements (or to be assertive in general) is the fact that you might be able to plant a seed in another person's head. You might not instantly get what you want, but maybe three months down the line, the situation arises where people remember that you wanted to do more of X and then invite you to do so. But this cannot happen unless they know what you want. Therefore, sometimes the simple act of letting people know what you want might just be a success in and of itself, a success that is under your control.

Reciprocity and concessions

Another great way of increasing the chances of other people saying yes to what you want is by using the principle of reciprocity – the old give and take. The idea is simple. Imagine you have just done someone a big favour and they are grateful for this. If you now need a favour from them, you have significantly increased the chances of this person helping you. People repay in kind (Cialdini, 2007).

Many examples highlight the powerful effect of reciprocity. For example, charities use it when sending out donation letters. Some of them include a little gift such as a pen, as they know that upon receiving a little gift, people feel more obliged to donate than without this little gift. A university professor decided to test the principle on a number of perfect strangers with Christmas cards. The results were overwhelming: a vast majority sent a card in return, without even questioning who he was (Kunz & Woolcott, 1976)!

The same principle also applies to the workplace. If you help your colleagues or your manager out, then the odds of them helping you in return significantly increase. Or in other words, the odds of them helping you shape your goals the way you want significantly increase. So, reciprocity is a very powerful tool when it comes to making sure that you get other people to say yes to the changes you want to make in relation to your goals. The power of this principle can be strengthened even more by the type of response you give when someone thanks you for the favour you did them. Rather than simply saying something like, "Sure, it's no big deal", a more influential response for guaranteeing future reciprocity is, "Sure, I know if the situation were ever reversed, you would do the same for me."

Another interesting twist in the context of reciprocity is the idea of concessions. Whenever you ask for a favour, start by asking for your ideal request. If this does not work, then you have the option to go down to a more moderate request. This principle works particularly when you have something to give, when you can show the other person that you are making a step towards them and willing to meet them halfway, although it does not need to be halfway all the time.

There is a famous study that best illustrates the power of concessions (Cialdini, 2007). Cialdini and his team went out in Phoenix, Arizona, and asked people if they would be willing to chaperone a group of juvenile delinquents to the zoo. Most people (83%) said no. They then used the power of concessions on a different group of people. Here they asked for a larger favour initially: would people be willing to spend two hours per week counselling a juvenile delinquent for the next two years? They all refused this request, as expected. Now Cialdini and his team applied their concession, i.e., having something to give, and asked if they could then chaperone a group of juvenile delinquents to the zoo for one day instead. Under these conditions, three times more people agreed! Remember, it was the same request, but the second group had one larger request put before it – just a few sentences dramatically increased the positive response to their initial request (day trip to the zoo).

An example in your work context could be regarding asking to work from home. Ideally, you would like two days a week. However, you would be happy with just one. The principle of concessions would suggest starting with two days. If the person in charge says no, then you have something to give – give up one day and try asking for one day instead. The same would apply to negotiations on salary.

There is a great heuristic Cialidini (2007) uses in this context. He says, if you retreat **in** the situation, you win; if you retreat **from** the situation, you lose. Retreating in the situation means if you can lower your request during (within) the negotiation, you increase your chances of success, i.e., getting what you want. Whereas, if you retreat from the situation, i.e., going away accepting the no, then you have obviously lost. But more importantly, if you leave the situation to reconsider your options and then come back a week later, this is seen as another completely different request, so the power of concessions will no longer apply. Therefore, the practical implications for any negotiations would be to ensure, before you even begin, that you have something to give during the negotiations.

One last thing to comment on in this context is ethics. Many people think it is manipulative, and it is true; you could use this principle in an unethical way. But you can also ensure you only use it in an ethical way by making sure your ideal request (e.g., two days), although ideal, is still a fair request. As long as it is fair, then it is not unethical; you are simply making a request for your ideal solution.

Broken record

The "broken record" technique is a very simple but useful one for times when negotiation is not working or not an option. If there is something you feel strongly about, sometimes all you can do is persistently insist with a repetitive statement. The technique consists of simply repeating your requests or your refusals every time you are met with resistance. The term comes from vinyl records, the surface of which, when scratched, would lead the needle

Table 10.2 Applying assertiveness to achieving your goals

My most important goals	Person to negotiate with for what I want more of within my goal	What techniques do I use? • I-statements • Reciprocity • Concessions	Person to negotiate with for what I want less of within my goal	What techniques do I use? • I-statements • Reciprocity • Concessions	When am I going to do this?
Goal 1					
Goal 2					
Goal 3					
Goal 4					

of a record player to loop over the same few seconds of the recording indefinitely. As with a broken record, the key to this approach is repetition.

To explain the use of the technique for making requests, imagine yourself talking to your manager about your work projects. Perhaps there is a particular project that you want to be given, or perhaps one that you would prefer to get rid of. When making requests, being a broken record is not literally repeating over and over, "I want this project. I want this project. I want this project." Instead, it is unrelentingly pushing your point with relevant information to argue your case. Rather than overwhelming your manager with a deluge of all your arguments upfront, state your request, "I would very much like to take on this project." Then bring out your arguments one by one as to why it is a good idea for your manager to give you the project until they eventually say yes. If things continue to not go your way, though, it is a good idea to have a backup plan using the above-mentioned concessions technique.

When using the technique to refuse someone else's request, it is also possible to give varying responses with your no response. If they continue to persist, then it is fine to stop providing arguments and simply repeat the word "no". However, there is one limiting factor to using this technique when saying no, you must be prepared to stand your ground. Think of a small child begging and pleading for a new toy. You say no a few times, but then give in. Aha – you have lost your power; the child knows that next time, if they play the broken record, they will eventually win!

Putting it all together

Putting all the assertiveness techniques together, we would like you to do the following exercise (see Table 10.2) to see with whom you need to have a conversation about reshaping your most important goals.

References

Cialdini, R. B. (2007). *Influence: The psychology of persuasion.* New York: HarperCollins Publishers.

Ehrlich, C. (2018). The development of an extended goal-striving reasons framework: Evidence for its relevance in the workplace, for its theoretical difference to self-concordance and for its buffering effect on work intensity. *Journal of Positive Psychology and Wellbeing*, 2(2), 1–23.

Ehrlich, C. (2019). The goal-striving reasons framework: Further evidence for its predictive power for subjective well-being on a sub-dimensional level and on an individual goal-striving reasons level as well as evidence for its theoretical difference to self-concordance. *Current Psychology, Online First*, 1–14.

Kunz, P. R., & Woolcott, M. (1976). Season's greetings: From my status to yours. *Social Science Research*, 5(3), 269–278. doi: 10.1016/0049-089X(76)90003-X

Chapter 11

Creativity/creative solutions

Many of the issues you will be reflecting on in relation to your goals will require you to find answers that are not necessarily obvious. Hopefully, the content of this book around goals will naturally lead to changes because you now have more specific information about which reasons for goal pursuit can increase happiness, which can decrease it, and why this is the case. However, with some of the topics we presented in this book, you might not find the solution straight away for a variety of reasons. One main reason is that applying concepts to yourself is sometimes much harder than helping someone else do the same. Therefore, for some solutions, you need to think outside the box. You need to come up with and try new, creative solutions. This is the reason for including this chapter on creativity. It covers some basic techniques that you might find useful when you get stuck and are finding it difficult to come up with any good ideas on how to modify a certain goal.

Going for a walk

Getting yourself in a creative mode is always possible but sometimes difficult. It is not something you can force yourself into. Often this is simply because you are trying too hard. Once you start to tense up, perhaps get a little anxious and/or stressed, the mind seems to erect a mental barrier. Creativity tends to flow when you are relaxed and often when not even focussed on the problem you are trying to solve. This is the basis for the phrase "sleep on it" when looking for novel solutions.

Research has shown that one extremely easy way to create a situation in which one can become more creative is to go for a walk (Oppezzo & Schwarz, 2014). When you are consciously occupied with other things, new ideas are more likely to pop into your head, and walking, particularly outdoors, has been found to be most helpful in stimulating creativity.

Once the ideas pop up, it is helpful to capture those ideas immediately so as not to forget them by the time you return to your desk. Therefore, carrying a small writing pad is useful, but a journaling app on your mobile phone is equally viable and probably even easier; it is the one gadget most people have with them most of the time. Also, the ideas can be easily stored and probably easier to find again, even after a few months.

Mind maps

Mind maps are a traditional "thinking outside the box" method of getting creative. Popularised by Tony Buzan and marketed as "the ultimate thinking tool" (Buzan, 2005), they work by letting your mind wander freely and explore things in all directions. Mind maps harness two keys: imagination and association.

We believe that the mind mapping technique is extremely useful when it comes to applying the knowledge on how to pursue your goals for the right reasons for your own situation. In essence, mind maps help you to answer some of the "How do I do this?" questions you might have had when working through this book. Often it is one thing to understand the theory, but a much more difficult thing to apply it to your specific situation. You might be thinking thoughts similar to these:

*   I know I would enjoy my goal more if it were more challenging for me. But how do I build more challenges into my goal?
*   I know and I agree with the argument that I should build in more pleasurable activities into my weekly routines. But I am very busy, and there are my kids, etc., that need so much time from me. How can I do this?
*   I know helping others is a good thing and doing this would increase my happiness, but how do I integrate helping others in a goal that has little to do with others?

To construct a mind map, start with writing the key idea or question in the middle and drawing a circle around it. Draw lines (branches) out from that circle and write the keywords that pop into your head. From each branch, draw sub-branches to write down the associations that pop into your mind from those initial keywords. As a basic example, you might start with the word "Goals". Possible branches out might include "personal goals", "professional goals", and "health goals". Sub-branches from the professional goals could include "targets to achieve" and "skills to improve", among others. "Skills to improve" could lead to things like "IT skills" and "presentation skills", and so on. The number of branches and sub-branches are determined simply by the number of things that come to mind.

Let us look at a couple of mind mapping examples for two "how do I do this" questions.

Example 1 (from Christian Ehrlich): For many years, I struggled to enjoy writing academic papers, which, as you can imagine, is not a good thing for an academic. I really enjoyed my teaching (and still do) but writing a paper was always a bit of a drag for me. And for a long time, although I was familiar with and firmly believed in the power of aligning your goals to your implicit motives (motives of the heart; see Chapter 7), I could not figure out a way of changing how I wrote papers so as to enjoy the process of doing it. I knew that my achievement motive and my power motive are the strongest drivers for me. So, I started a mind map on the question: how can I change the way I write so it aligns better with my power motive? In the first instance, I started to think of all the different ways the power motive could be expressed (the branches). Then I started to fill each of the branches (influencing others, helping others, having more of an impact on others) with possible solutions. Finally, one of the ideas around influencing really made a difference for me. It was about really putting myself into the readers' shoes so that I could think carefully about the best way to present my arguments to convince my readers as much as possible. I now enjoy writing a lot more than before. But to be honest, this process took about two years to figure exactly what I needed to be doing to enjoy writing more. In the end, it needed a spark of an idea that was not obvious to me for a long time. Mind mapping really helped here because it created new ideas on how to express my power motives in three different ways (influencing, helping, and increasing my power base/status), which I then followed up with potential options and, luckily, the idea of trying to persuade/influence the reader worked.

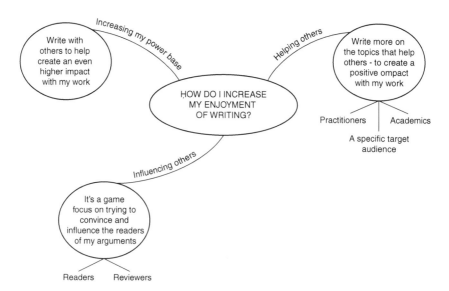

Figure 11.1 Mind map on matching implicit and explicit goals – Example 1: increasing enjoyment of writing.

Example 2 (from Sashenka Milston): I have always loved reading. I was the child curled up under my covers with a flashlight after bed-time, never wanting to put my latest book down. As an adult, I found that life got in the way. I still bought books with great interest in and intention of reading them, but my bookshelves and bedside became littered with unread books. I just could not find the time to read any-more! So, I started a mind map on how to find time to include the simple pleasure of reading in my life again. For this exercise, I felt that the achievement motive might a good one to tap in to. In my case, my implicit achievement motive is one of avoidance, so I needed to figure out how to take all the pressure off. Through a new understanding of my implicit motives, I realised that I had subconsciously put up some barriers in the form of needing to read – rather than wanting to read – to get through the backlog of books. Of course, when something becomes a chore, it takes away the pleasure and creates resistance to performing the task! After coming to this realisation – that it was not something I needed to accomplish, but instead, a pleasurable escape – a cascade of thoughts was triggered, and I was able to find little pockets of time. As a result, I am now finding great pleasure in my little mo-ments of reading dotted through my week.

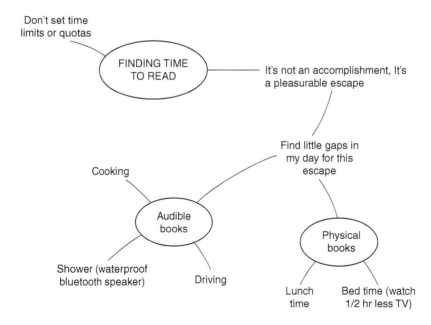

Figure 11.2 Mind map on matching implicit and explicit goals – Example 2: finding time to read.

Please keep in mind that mind mapping is a creative activity, so do not place any limitations on your thinking during the mind mapping process; let the ideas blossom and flow in any direction. You can build in relevant realistic constraints later when you are making a final plan, but if you curtail your thinking beforehand, you might miss some viable solutions that you would not normally have thought of.

Asking others for help/getting coached

Another important factor that can help you in modifying your goals is asking others for help or for their view on things. This might also provide some further ideas on what you could potentially try out. The person you talk to could be anyone: a family member, a friend, a work colleague, or even a stranger! In fact, there is a whole industry that specialises in helping people with things like this; the coaching industry's sole purpose is to help people to solve their own problems.

It is also a fact that sometimes just talking about things can clarify thoughts and help with problem solving. How many times have you found yourself coming up with a solution before you even finished explaining the problem to someone? Thinking aloud has been well-documented as aiding problem solving (Ahlum-heath & DiVesta, 1986; Berry, 1983; Ericsson & Simon, 1993). Research suggests that thinking aloud helps to identify strategies to improve understanding (Israel & Massey, 2005). There are also other benefits to communicating out loud as opposed to silently thinking as you engage more areas of your brain. Communicating feelings has been shown to reduce emotional reactivity (Lieberman et al., 2007), which is useful as emotions can suppress reasoning (Oaksford et al., 1996). Talking out loud can help you stay focussed and significantly increase the amount of control during challenging tasks (Kirkham et al., 2012). Self-talk training in athletes has been shown to reduce anxiety and increase self-confidence and performance (Walter et al., 2019) – think about the tennis players you see talking to themselves or yelling, "Come on!" after each point.

So, give it a try. The next time you have a problem to solve, find someone to talk to about it. See if, through a discussion or simply talking at them, you discover new ideas on how to solve your problem. And if you can't find anyone else, talk out loud to yourself!

References

Ahlum-heath, M. E., & DiVesta, F. J. (1986). The effects of conscious controlled verbalization of a cognitive strategy on transfer in problem solving. *Memory and Cognition, 14*, 281–285. doi: 10.3758/BF03197704

Berry, D. C. (1983). Metacognitive experience and transfer of logical reasoning. *Quarterly Journal of Experimental Psychology, 35A*(1), 39–49. doi: 10.1080/14640748308402115

Buzan, T. (2005). *Mind map handbook*. London: Thorsons.

Ericsson, K. A., & Simon, H. A. (1993). *Protocol analysis: Verbal reports as data* (revised edition). Cambridge, MA: MIT Press.

Israel, S., & Massey, D. D. (2005). Think alouds as a means for building metacognition with middle schoolers. In C. C. Block, S. E. Israel, K. Kinnucan-Welsch, & K. L. Bauserman (Eds.), *Metacognition and literacy learning* (pp. 183–199). Mahwah, NJ: Erlbaum.

Kirkham, A. J., Breeze, J. M., & Mari-Beffa, P. (2012). The impact of verbal instructions on goal-directed behaviour. *Acta Psychologica, 139*(1), 212–219. doi: 10.1016/j.actpsy.2011.09.016

Lieberman, M. D., Eisenberger, N. I., Crockett, M. J., Tom, S. M., Pfeiffer, J. H., & Way, B. M. (2007). Putting feelings into words: Affect labeling disrupts amygdala activity in response to affective stimuli. *Psychology Science, 18*(5), 421–427. doi: 10.1111/j.1467-9280.2007.01916.x

Oaksford, M., Morris, F., Grainger, B., & Williams, J. M. G. (1996). Mood, reasoning, and central executive processes. *Journal of Experimental Psychology: Learning, Memory, and Cognition, 22*(2), 476–492. doi: 10.1037/0278-7393.22.2.476

Oppezzo, M., & Schwartz, D. L. (2014). Give your ideas some legs: The positive effect of walking on creative thinking. *Journal of Experimental Psychology – Learning Memory and Cognition, 40*(4), 1142–1152. doi: 10.1037/a0036577

Walter, N., Nikoleizig, L., & Alfermann, D. (2019). Effects of self-talk training on competitive anxiety, self-efficacy, volitional skills, and performance: An intervention study with junior sub-elite athletes. *Sports, 7*(6), 148. doi: 10.3390/sports7060148

Chapter 12

Summary

This book ultimately focused on one fundamental question: why are you pursuing your most important goals in life? This question is so fundamental because the answers you give yourself can make an impactful difference to your happiness. Based on the goal-striving reasons framework, you were introduced to four important reasons for goal pursuit: pleasure, altruism, self-esteem, and necessity. The relevance of each of these reasons is supported by a vast amount of research. For each reason, we provided various strategies for increasing the amount of pleasure or altruism in our goals and reducing the extent to which we pursue our goals out of self-esteem and necessity.

We hope that the information in this book led to some instant changes. Equally, some of the exercises or concepts in this book are not always that easy to apply to your own life. So, don't be too harsh on yourself if, even though you understood the theoretical concept, it has not clicked yet and has not led to an improvement in your goal-striving reasons, or indeed happiness. For example, it took me (Chris) a couple of years (!) to figure out how to link my goal of becoming a better academic writer to my implicit motives. This is despite the fact that I had no doubt that the concept – aligning my actions with my implicit motives – would be the key to enjoying my writing a lot more. This is why we included the chapter on creativity. Sometimes we need a new idea on how to apply things to our own situation, and these ideas often come up when we least expect them. The main thing is to persist, to keep circling around the issue, and to not give up until, eventually, you have an idea that cracks it and makes a significant change to the reason why you pursue a certain goal.

Equally, the notion of conditional self-esteem is ingrained in our society. Many people have this view and a great deal of the information we are given, such as through marketing campaigns and advertising, unfortunately perpetuates this kind of self-esteem. (Otherwise, people would not buy as much!) Therefore, our persistence is necessary here too, along with sheer will, to avoid being overly influenced by those messages and to start to believe that unconditional self-esteem is one of the keys to our happiness.

We hope you have found this book useful and that it has led to changes regarding your goal-striving reasons, not least because positive changes in people's goal-striving reasons go hand-in-hand with higher levels of happiness. We also hope that this book becomes a useful go-to place when you are struggling with your happiness and where you can pick up useful ideas on how to continue improving your happiness in the future.

Index

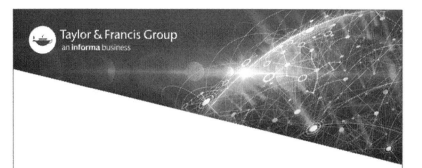

Printed in Great Britain
by Amazon

78886365R00045